P9-DFR-021

The International Business Environment

The International Business Environment

A Management Guide

Harold J. Heck

American Management Association, Inc.

This book has been distributed without charge to AMA members enrolled in the International Management Division.

Library of Congress catalog card number: 68–57856

Foreword

In the past two decades many American companies have "gone international" for the first time. Whatever may have impelled this in individual cases, it is highly probable that any one of several important developments affecting the background and conduct of international business which occurred in the postwar period may have been a contributing factor.

Among those developments whose impact gave rise to a much wider American interest in international business than ever existed before on the part of both businessmen and academicians are the following:

1. The appearance of several new or updated *international* economic institutions, some appearing as intergovernmental agreements or treaties, and some as actual, formal establishments.
2. The breakup of empires and the emergence of many new nations, all of which clamor for rapid, if not immediate, economic development, and many of which attempt to attract foreign investment by tax "breaks" or other incentives.
3. The emergence of several new discriminatory or preferential trading areas in which American exporters are at a competitive disadvantage as compared with those within the area.
4. The development of and increased activity in intergovernmental commodity trading arrangements involving an impressive segment of merchandise trade.
5. A continued trend toward the opening up of foreign markets by means of negotiating away trade obstacles, but an unwillingness so far to adopt a multilaterally agreed set of policies covering international trading relations.
6. A modification in attitudes toward private restrictive business practices, such as cartels and price-fixing arrangements, especially in the major industrial countries.

7. A large increase in the volume of international trade throughout the world ($192 billion of imports in 1966 as compared with only $34 billion in 1946).
8. A large increase in international investment and licensing activities ($55 billion of U.S. direct investments in 1966 as against $12 billion in 1950; and $60 billion of foreign-owned assets in the United States in 1966 as compared with $18 billion in 1950).
9. An increase in the overall net U.S. creditor position (from $14 billion in 1950 to $52 billion in 1966).

These are the types of phenomena that influence and even create the environment in which international business must be conducted and through which international business opportunities become attractive to individual firms. They are an important source of the difference between purely domestic and international business.

It is the purpose of this book to identify and study some of the major economic and legal institutions that differentiate domestic and international business and that bear directly on the latter. Not all international economic organizations are discussed; information pertaining to organizations as such is available in publications such as *World Economic Agencies,* by C. H. Alexandrowicz (Frederick A. Praeger, 1964); the *Yearbook of International Organizations* (published by the Union of International Associations, in official collaboration with the United Nations); and *Europa Yearbook,* Volume I (published by Europa Publications, Ltd., London). International businessmen must often be informed about these institutions, however, which are several in number, some being highly specialized.

Of course, laws, regulations, and even organizations are subject to constant change through amendment, replacement, or demise. So treatment of them is not to be considered as definitive and indefinitely valid, but as explanatory and indicative of the several intangible forces affecting international business decisions every day.

Finally, this book does not attempt to tell anyone how to do business internationally, neither does it relate to the adequacy or suitability of a company's own resources or its products, nor does it pertain to internal company organization. Rather it serves to acquaint the reader with the general environment within which international business is conducted, and especially the elements of such environment over which an individual firm has little or no control, but to which it may have to adjust.

HAROLD J. HECK

Contents

Chapter I

Principal Trading Nations and Products in World Trade

An appropriate introduction to international business is to recognize some of the dimensions of the subject within an overall picture of the principal trading nations of the world and the products which make up most of the world's commerce. As one should expect, some countries are more important as world traders than others. Some are more involved in foreign trade than others because of the nature of their resources, their proximity to trading partners, their size, and the structure of their economies. This chapter identifies the mainstream and forces of commodity trade bearing on the workings of the international economy. To give a picture of this, Exhibits 1–4 have been designed.

The first of these exhibits pertains to international trade by country. The tabulation, which includes all the countries that either export or import as much as one-half of 1 percent of the world total, shows that the trade of the entire world is dominated by only a few nations, of which five contribute almost 45 percent of the total of exports and absorb over 42 percent of the world's imports. The top ten countries provide almost two-thirds of the world's exports and absorb almost as large a proportion of its imports. We have therefore a possibility of conflict in attitude toward foreign trade policy between those countries that are most immediately active in foreign trade and those that are not so involved, worldwide, but that are perhaps quite dependent on it for their viability as well as for their economic development.

EXHIBIT 1

PRINCIPAL TRADING NATIONS OF THE WORLD, 1966

	Exports ($ billion)	*Percent of Total*	*Imports ($ billion)*	*Percent of Total*
United States	30.3	16.70	27.3	14.22
West Germany	19.3	10.64	17.4	9.06
United Kingdom	14.1	7.77	15.9	8.28
France	10.4	5.73	11.5	5.99
Japan	9.2	5.07	8.8	4.59
Canada	9.0	4.96	9.3	4.84
Italy	7.6	4.19	8.0	4.17
Belgium-Luxembourg	6.7	3.69	7.0	3.65
Netherlands	6.6	3.63	7.8	4.08
Sweden	4.1	2.26	4.3	2.25
Switzerland	3.2	1.76	3.8	1.98
Australia	3.0	1.65	3.5	1.82
Venezuela	2.7	1.49	1.3	0.68
Union of Soviet Socialist Reps.	2.5	1.38	2.6	1.35
Denmark	2.4	1.32	2.9	1.51
South Africa	1.7	0.94	2.5	1.30
Brazil	1.6	0.88	1.4	0.73
Saudi Arabia	1.5	0.83	0.6	0.31
Norway	1.5	0.83	2.3	1.20
China (Mainland)	1.4	0.77	1.5	0.78
Austria	1.4	0.77	2.1	1.09
Argentina	1.4	0.77	1.1	0.57
Kuwait	1.3	0.72	0.4	0.21
Hong Kong	1.3	0.72	1.3	0.68
India	1.3	0.72	2.5	1.30
Iran	1.3	0.72	0.9	0.47
Finland	1.2	0.66	1.4	0.73
Mexico	1.2	0.66	1.6	0.83
Spain	1.1	0.61	3.5	1.82
New Zealand	1.1	0.61	1.1	0.57
Libya	1.0	0.55	0.4	0.21
Malaysia	1.0	0.55	0.7	0.36
Iraq	0.9	0.50	0.4	0.21
Poland	0.9	0.50	1.0	0.52
Chile	0.9	0.50	0.7	0.36
Philippines	0.8	0.44	1.0	0.52
Yugoslavia	0.8	0.44	1.1	0.57
Thailand	0.7	0.38	1.2	0.63
Ireland	0.6	0.33	1.0	0.62
Portugal	0.6	0.33	1.0	0.52
Greece	0.3	0.17	1.1	0.57
Residual	21.5	11.86	26.8	13.95

Source: *Direction of Trade*, International Bank for Reconstruction and Development, International Monetary Fund, Washington, D.C., Annual 1962-1966, pp. 3-9.

The leading exporters are also the leading importers, substantially in order of export rank. On the other hand, there are numerous countries whose foreign trade is less than 1 percent of the world's total. As a matter of fact, only about 20 countries individually account for that high a percentage. This characteristic of relative trading importance is significant in international economic relations, especially in the negotiation and establishment of agreements and organizations, wherein pressure is strong for one-man, one-vote.

DIRECTION OF TRADE

Exhibit 2 is a percentage arrangement of the directional flow of exports originating in selected areas, groupings, and from one country, Japan. Immediately one notes the workings of proximity, as reflected in the high concentration of export trade by Western Europe with itself, of the European Economic Community (EEC) and the European Free Trade Association (EFTA) within themselves and with each other, and of the two regional groups with Western Europe, of which they are part. Exhibit 2 also reflects the East-West tensions and restrictions in that 60 percent of Eastern Trading Zone exports went to other members of the same trading zone.

Western Europe exports just about 10 percent of its total to North America, while almost a third of North America's total goes to Western Europe. The same disparity appears in the importance to each other of North America and EEC and EFTA.

The importance of the industrial areas both as exporters and as a market for the exports of both the industrial and the developing areas is apparent, as are the relative unimportance of eastern areas in world trade and the fact that the developing areas do not find their major markets among themselves, but in the industrial countries.

PRINCIPAL COMMODITIES

One of the main difficulties in seeking worldwide commodity trade data is that not all countries report on the same classification system; those that do, do not all report in the same detail or with equal promptness. Yet within these limitations some statistics have been drawn up to give a feeling of the relative importance of products or product groupings that make up world trade.

In commodity aggregates, the best published tabulation appears to be that

EXHIBIT 2

DIRECTIONAL FLOW OF REGIONAL TRADE, 1966
(Percent of exporter totals)

Destination:

Exporting Area:	*North America*	*Western Europe*	*EEC*	*EFTA*	*Japan*	*Latin America*	*Southeast Asia*	*Africa*	*Total Developing Areas**	*Australia New Zealand South Africa*	*Eastern Trading Zone*	*Total ($ billion)*
North America	32.6	28.8	14.9	10.6	7.0	11.8	7.9	2.5	26.2	3.5	2.0	37.1
Western Europe	10.3	64.1	37.0	20.7	0.9	3.5	3.5	5.1	15.9	3.5	4.9	86.5
EEC	8.8	69.1	44.1	19.0	0.8	3.5	2.9	5.5	15.2	1.8	3.8	52.7
EFTA	13.2	55.8	25.2	22.5	1.1	3.4	4.9	4.8	18.2	7.2	4.4	28.0
Japan	33.4	13.3	6.0	5.4	—	4.7	26.9	3.0	38.9	5.0	6.1	9.8
Latin America	35.7	32.3	19.8	9.1	4.7	9.9	6.5	5.5	18.8	0.3	8.2	11.6
Southeast Asia	19.8	23.3	11.2	10.5	13.3	1.1	24.2	3.2	31.9	3.2	8.7	9.8
Africa	8.6	67.5	46.0	18.5	2.5	0.6	2.4	7.6	12.4	1.6	6.7	8.3
Total Developing Areas	20.9	40.7	24.5	13.2	8.1	3.9	8.1	3.3	20.7	2.1	6.3	38.8
Australia, New Zealand, South Africa	15.5	45.1	16.9	26.1	13.9	0.7	6.7	4.4	16.6	5.3	3.4	5.7
Eastern Trading Zone	1.1	19.9	8.4	6.7	2.5	3.4	5.9	3.0	13.8	0.2	60.1	23.1

* Includes developing countries and territories which do not belong to the areas specified.

Source: Developed from Table A in appendix to *International Trade*, 1966, published by GATT, 1967.

prepared by the Statistical Office of the United Nations, on the basis of Standard International Trade Classification (SITC) one-digit sections. This is shown in Exhibit 3, and it will be seen that world trade, by value, is heavily concentrated in manufactured goods—over 50 percent of the total. Primary commodities, such as food, beverages, and tobacco, and oils and fats,

EXHIBIT 3

COMPOSITION OF WORLD EXPORTS, BY SITC SECTION
($ billion)

SITC Section		*1961*	*1962*	*1963*	*1964*	*1965*	*1966*
0 – 1	Food, beverages, and tobacco	23.4	24.5	27.3	30.0	31.0	32.9
2 – 4	Crude materials, excluding fuels, oils, and fats	21.1	20.6	22.0	23.9	24.7	26.2
3	Mineral fuels and related materials	13.5	14.5	15.7	17.0	17.9	19.1
5	Chemicals	7.9	8.5	9.4	10.9	12.2	13.7
7	Machinery and transport equipment	30.1	33.2	36.4	40.9	45.7	51.5
6 – 8	Other manufactured goods	35.9	37.9	41.0	47.0	51.7	56.9

Source: *Monthly Bulletin of Statistics*, United Nations, March 1965, March 1967, and March 1968.

make up about 30 percent, and mineral fuels represent about 10 percent of the total. It can also be noted that the larger growth in recent years has been in manufactured goods, a circumstance which spokesmen for the developing countries sometimes cite as placing them at an increasing disadvantage *relative* to the developed areas.

When it comes to narrowing down to smaller groupings or even to individual commodities, the Statistical Office of the United Nations reports that until early 1968 it had made no such computations. A detailed tabulation of world trade in primary commodities was prepared for the United Nations Conference on Trade and Development in 1964.[1] These items were selected

[1] *Trade and Development, Commodity Trade,* United Nations Publication, Sales No. 64. II.B. 13, 1965, pp. 61–64.

because, at the conference, attention was focused on trade in primary commodities since they are the main output of the less-developed nations and are imported primarily by industrial nations. However, by omitting trade in manufactured goods, an incomplete and biased picture of the product composition of world trade results.

To modify this shortcoming, especially in view of the fact that the purpose of the tabulation is not statistical precision down to the last digit as much as a reasonable identification of the major items that compose world trade, Exhibit 4 has been developed from export and import statistics of the Organization for Economic Cooperation and Development (OECD) countries.[2] These countries, whose statistics make up the total, represent the principal trading nations of the world,[3] but, even so, the statistics are incomplete in that they do not include goods moving between nonreporting countries—for example, between Brazil and Mexico, India and South Africa, or the Soviet Union and Poland. But they do include exports moving from the OECD countries to the nonreporting ones—for example, from the United States to the several Latin American countries and from the several European countries to the African countries; and they do include imports originating in Latin America and Africa and other nonreporting countries and going into Western Europe and North America.

It will be seen that quite a number of the large-volume commodities reported in Exhibit 4 individually account for 1 percent or more of total world trade. Not only that, commodities as well as countries swing weight, so to speak. For example, the leading ten commodities imported into and exported from the reporting countries represent over 20 percent of *total* world imports and exports, respectively. Attention is also drawn by the fact that several primary commodities, world trade in which moves typically from developing to industrial areas, each represent close to $2 billion of foreign exchange earnings for their producers—for example, petroleum, copper, coffee, wool, and ores and concentrates of nonferrous base metals.

In many cases trade in these products constitutes the major source of foreign exchange earnings to a nation. This poses a particular problem when (1) prices and volumes of primary commodities fluctuate more than do prices of manufactured goods which these developing nations wish to buy, and (2) many of these primary commodities are produced in developed as well as developing countries and in some cases are subject to import restric-

[2] Austria, Belgium-Luxembourg, Canada, Denmark, France, Germany, Greece, Iceland, Ireland, Italy, Japan, Netherlands, Norway, Portugal, Spain, Sweden, Switzerland, Turkey, United Kingdom, United States, and Yugoslavia.

[3] Over 70 percent of total world exports and imports, as reported by the United Nations.

tions in the developed countries. Therefore, developing countries are actively seeking preferences in trading opportunities for the goods they are able to produce.

COMPOSITION AND POSITION OF U.S. FOREIGN TRADE

The foreign trade of the United States means many things to many people, and there are several viewpoints from which it may be examined. Perhaps the first is in terms of volume—$31 billion of exports and $27 billion of imports for the United States in 1967. Another is the proportion of exports to Gross National Product (GNP) or to the production of movable goods—about 8 to 9 percent. The latter is a more meaningful indicator of the importance of exports to the economy, since the base excludes services, construction, and such activities that could not, in any case, be exported. Other significant characteristics of our foreign trade are its composition by product, by country, and finally by the role played by the United States in the foreign trade of other countries.

EXPORTS AND IMPORTS, BY SITC SECTIONS

SITC sections are aggregates of the most detailed classification that has been agreed internationally (see Appendix A). These aggregates are only of recent availability, so it is not possible to develop a long-term trend of U.S. foreign trade arranged in these categories. However, the Department of Commerce has reworked some of its earlier statistics to provide a needed time series and a bridge over to the new arrangement, and data are available for a decade or so. Beginning with 1957, Exhibits 5–12 indicate the dollar value of exports and imports according to these broad groupings. In most cases, as an aid to better understanding, the most important products falling within the section are listed.

An examination of these Exhibits points up a number of salient characteristics of U.S. foreign trade. Among these are:

1. U.S. foreign trade interest, productwise, is not heavily concentrated; an important export and import interest (say, above $1–2 billion) is observable in most of the major categories, although some of the groupings are *relatively* unimportant.
2. In several groupings, exports and imports are reasonably equal in total value. This is the case with our foreign trade in food and

(*Text continues on page 26.*)

EXHIBIT 4

LEADING COMMODITIES IN WORLD TRADE, 1966
(Based on foreign trade of OECD countries)

	Reported Exports	*Report[ed] Import[s]*
	($ million)	
Road motor vehicles	10,520	7,013
Petroleum, crude and partly refined	314	8,449
Machinery and appliances – nonelectrical – parts	7,678	4,878
Petroleum products	2,437	3,740
Copper	1,285	3,580
Power generating machinery, other than electrical	2,924	1,904
Other electrical machinery and apparatus	2,822	2,071
Wheat – including spelt and meslin, unmilled	2,694	1,099
Universals, plates, and sheets of iron or steel	2,634	1,919
Organic chemicals	2,545	1,893
Paper and paperboard	2,507	2,458
Machines for special industries	2,500	1,530
Clothing, except fur clothing	2,279	2,380
Fresh fruit and nuts – excluding oil nuts	1,029	2,337
Textile fabrics, woven (excluding narrow, specifically not cotton)	2,315	1,856
Coffee	73	2,259
Telecommunications apparatus	2,251	1,416
Ships and boats	2,156	880
Meat, fresh, chilled, or frozen	939	2,148
Wool and other animal hair	505	2,137
Plastic materials, regenerated cellulose, and artificial resins	2,058	1,477
Aircraft	2,054	1,095
Electric power machinery and switchgear	1,994	1,348
Iron ore and concentrates	728	1,961
Scientific, medical, and so forth, measuring instruments and apparatus	1,912	1,437
Ores and concentrates of nonferrous base metals	571	1,905
Wood, shaped, or simply worked	1,047	1,863

EXHIBIT 4

(continued)	*Reported Exports*	*Reported Imports*
	($ million)	
ice machines	1,847	1,642
xtile yarn and thread	1,838	1,297
icultural machinery and implements	1,831	1,351
xtile and leather machinery	1,779	1,063
-seeds, oil nuts, and oil kernels	973	1,731
al, coke, and briquettes	1,234	1,704
n and steel bars, rods, angles, shapes, sections	1,639	1,351
arls, precious and semiprecious stones	1,205	1,625
lp and waste paper	1,357	1,615
talworking machinery	1,534	1,069
ize (corn), unmilled	1,018	1,525
edstuff for animals (excluding unmilled cereals)	782	1,485
emical materials and products, not elsewhere specified	1,474	1,014
tton	664	1,472
dicinal and pharmaceutical products	1,419	825
bes, pipes, and fittings of iron or steel	1,352	761
ar and honey	195	1,338
oholic beverages	1,158	1,274
minum	1,254	1,159
od in the rough or roughly squared	312	1,230
getables, roots, and tubes, fresh or dried	785	1,205
earms of war and ammunition therefor	1,084	185
sh, fresh and simply preserved	793	1,053
rtilizers, manufactured	1,044	594
de rubber (including synthetic and reclaimed)	464	1,032
nufactures of metal, not elsewhere specified	998	744
nted matter	989	748
tton fabrics, woven (excluding narrow or specified fabrics)	979	732
bacco, unmanufactured	774	932
icles of rubber	825	556
mestic electrical equipment	807	587

rce: Developed from *Commodity Trade: Exports;* and *Commodity Trade: Imports*, Series C, Organization for Economic Cooperation and Development, January-December 1966.

EXHIBIT 5

UNITED STATES EXPORTS AND IMPORTS, 1957-67
(Food and live animals)

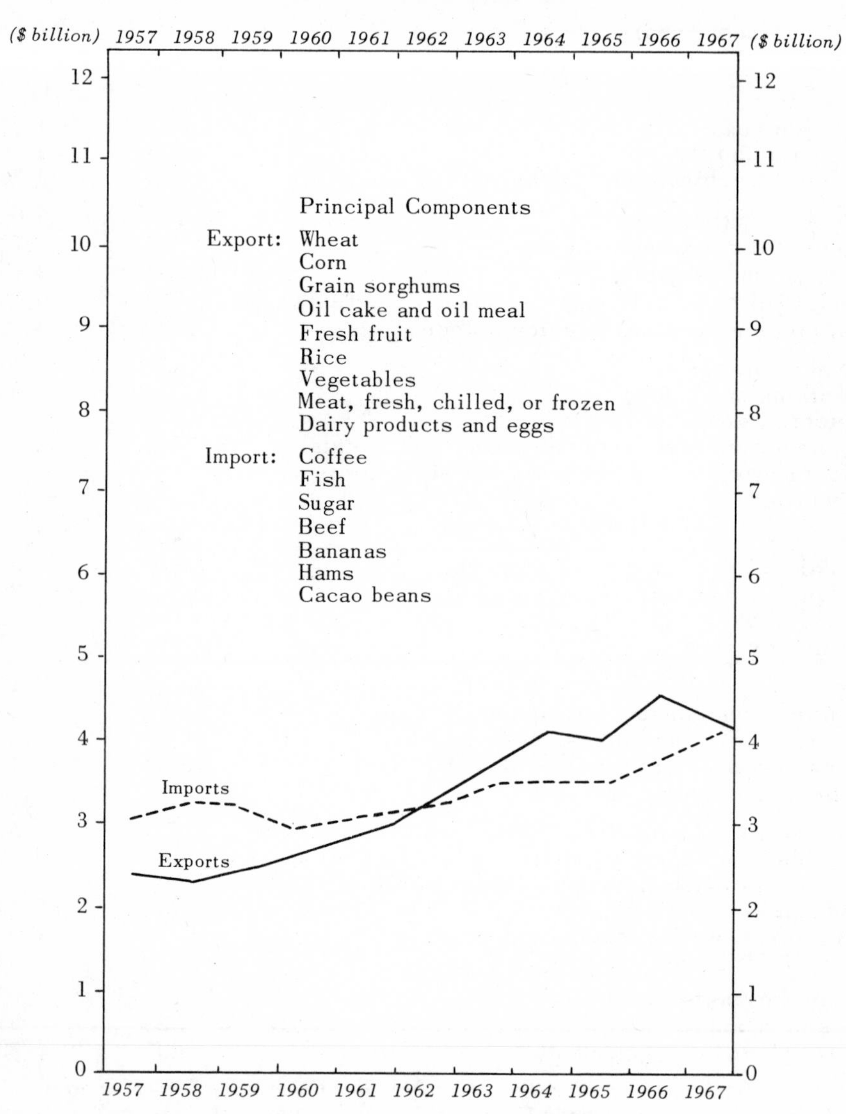

Data: ($ million)

1957	1958	1959	1960	1961	1962	1963	1964	1965	1966	1967
2,388	2,240	2,405	2,684	2,960	3,245	3,657	4,083	4,003	4,562	4,064
3,052	3,211	3,176	2,996	3,018	3,243	3,401	3,487	3,460	3,948	4,003

Note: The source of Exhibits 5-12 is as follows: *Overseas Business Reports* 65-60 and 67-43, 68-5, U. S. Department of Commerce, Washington, D. C., 1965, 1967, and 1968 respectively.

EXHIBIT 6

UNITED STATES EXPORTS AND IMPORTS 1957-67
(Beverages and tobacco)

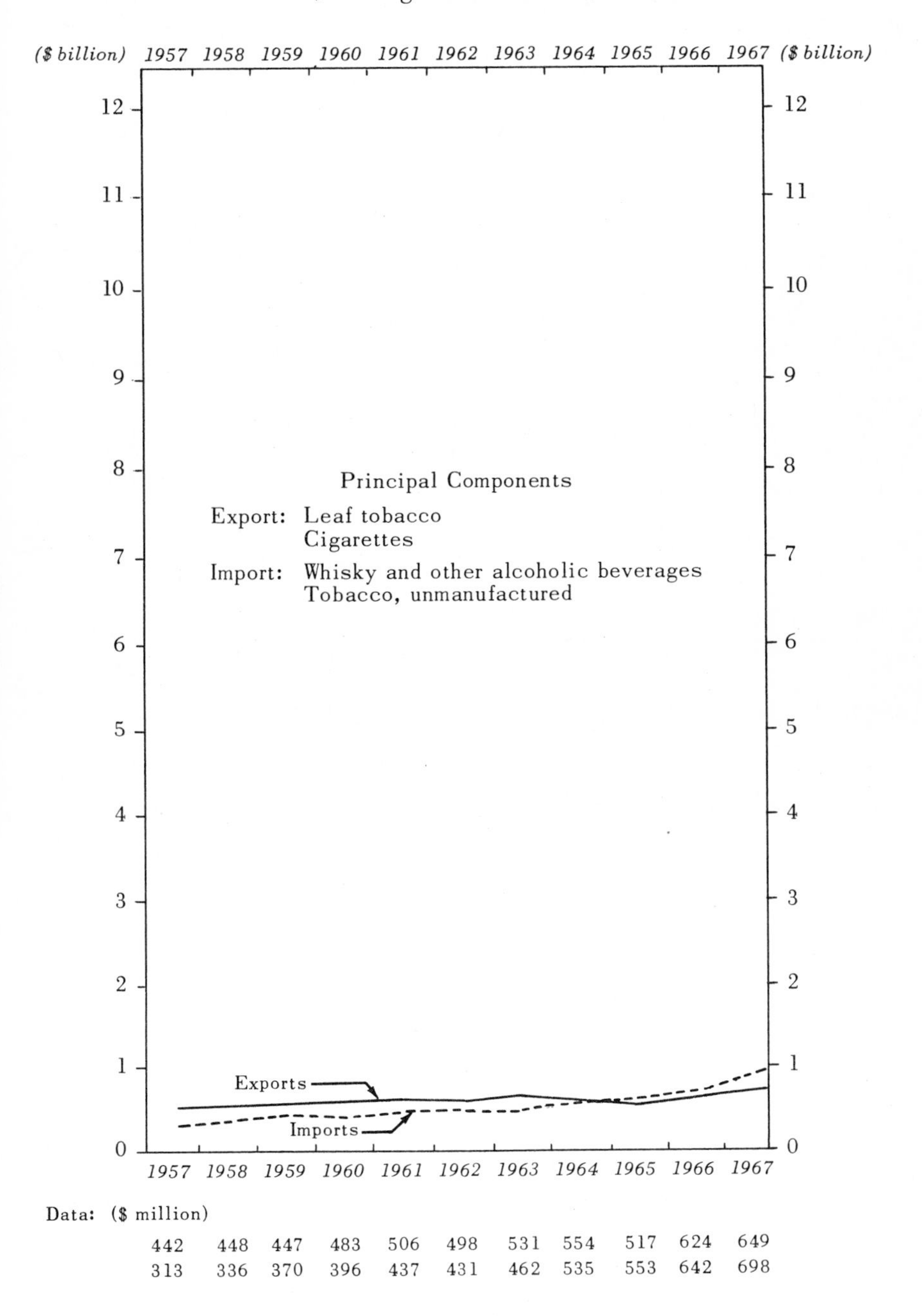

Data: ($ million)

1957	1958	1959	1960	1961	1962	1963	1964	1965	1966	1967
442	448	447	483	506	498	531	554	517	624	649
313	336	370	396	437	431	462	535	553	642	698

EXHIBIT 7

UNITED STATES EXPORTS AND IMPORTS 1957-67
(Crude materials, inedible, except fuels)

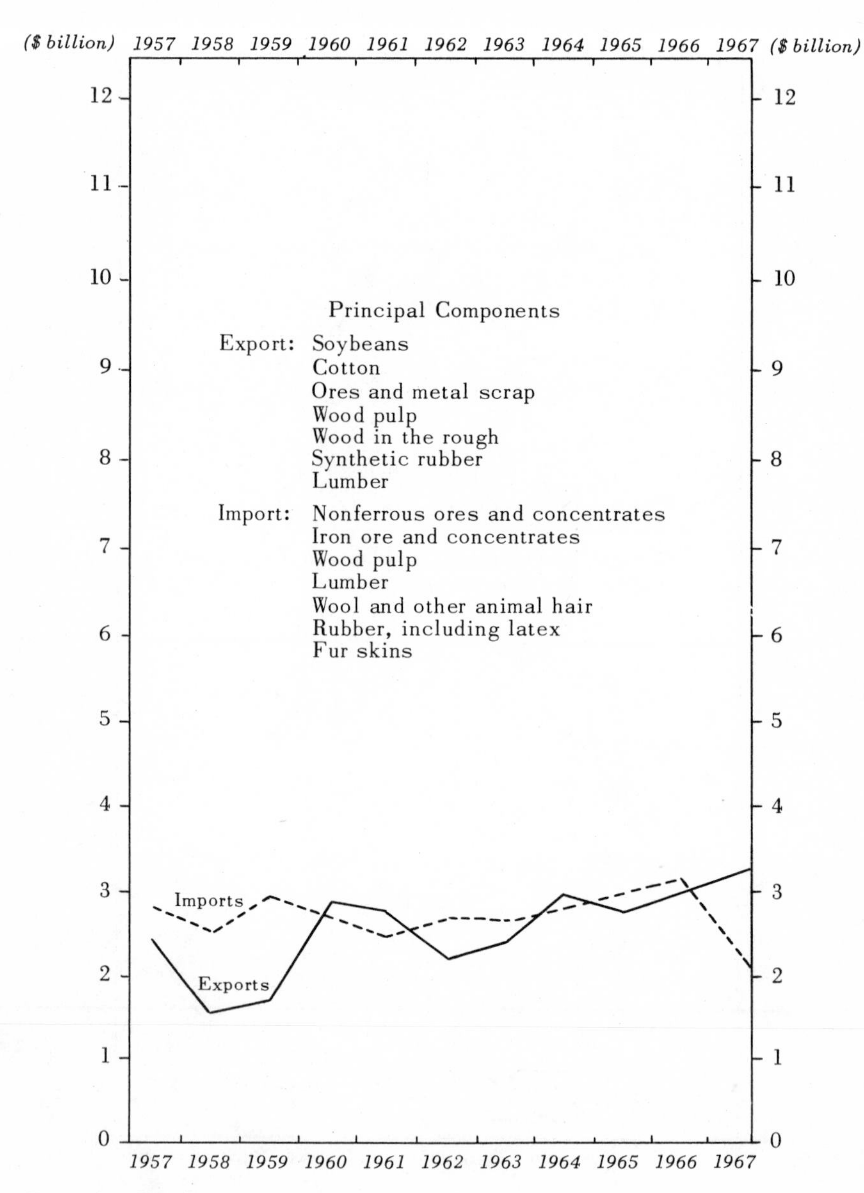

Data: ($ million)

2,533	1,708	1,823	2,805	2,794	2,226	2,493	2,969	2,855	3,070	3,280
2.766	2.365	2.925	2.711	2.485	2.668	2.673	2.827	3.047	3.266	2,965

EXHIBIT 8

UNITED STATES EXPORTS AND IMPORTS 1957-67
(Mineral fuels and related materials)

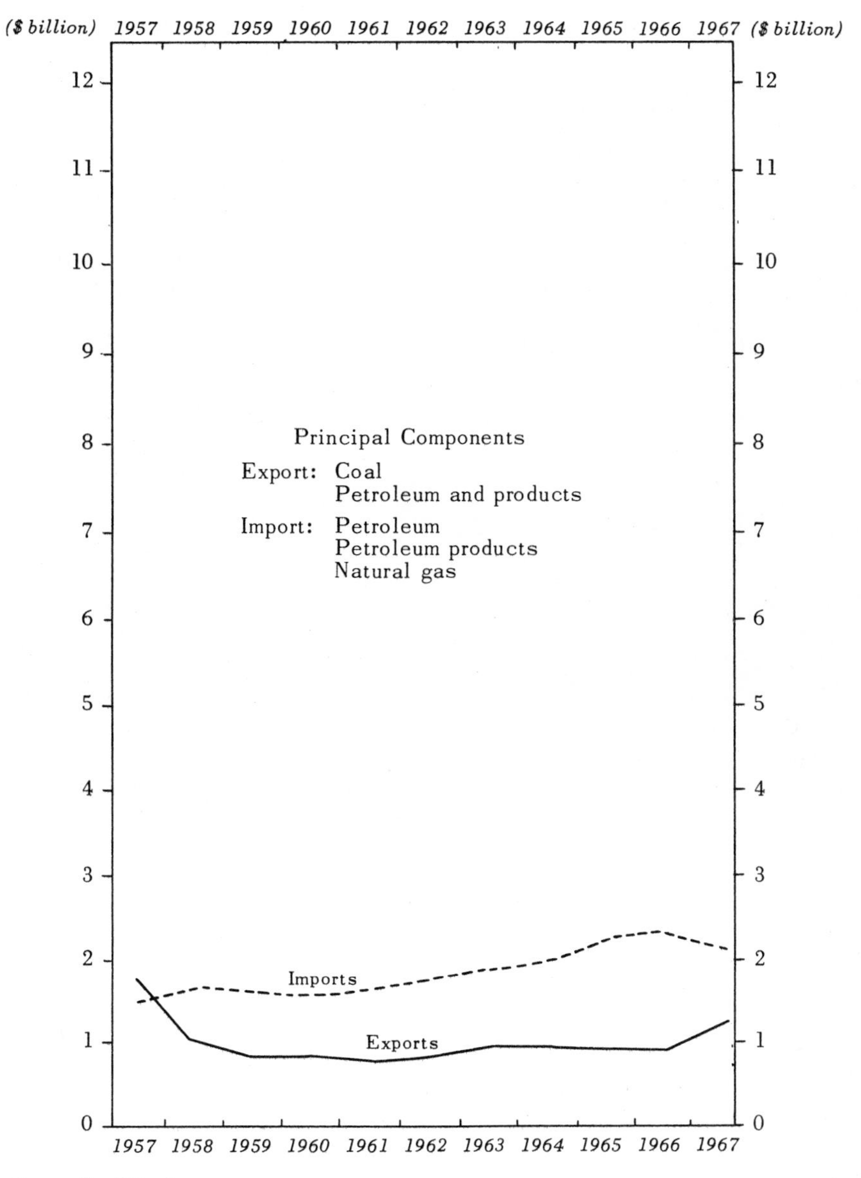

Data: ($ million)

1957	1958	1959	1960	1961	1962	1963	1964	1965	1966	1967
1,814	1,071	853	842	797	828	978	953	947	976	1,104
1.556	1.641	1.559	1.574	1.725	1.874	1.914	2.030	2.222	2.262	2.250

EXHIBIT 9

UNITED STATES EXPORTS AND IMPORTS 1957-67
(Animal and vegetable oils and fats)

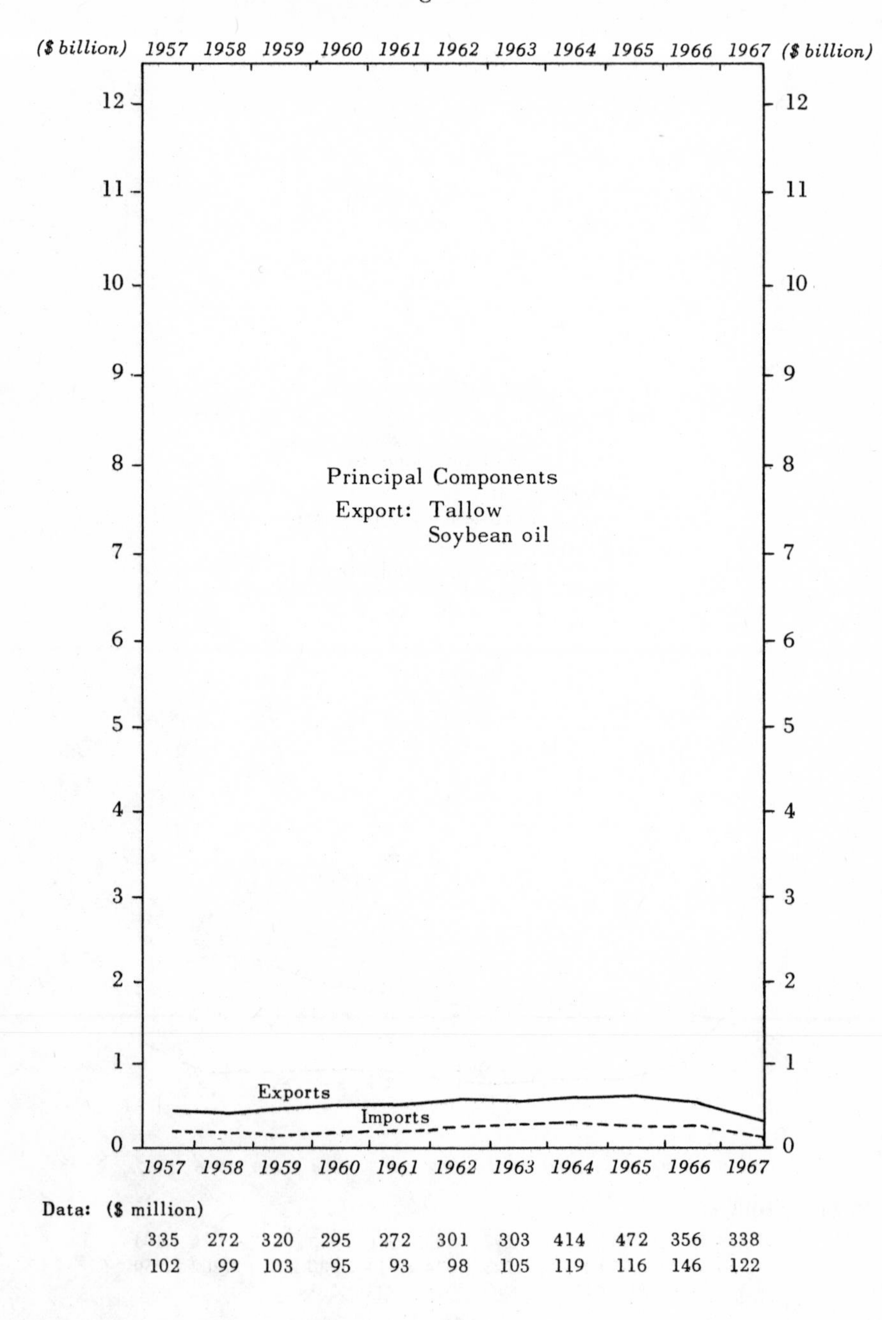

Data: ($ million)

	1957	1958	1959	1960	1961	1962	1963	1964	1965	1966	1967
Exports	335	272	320	295	272	301	303	414	472	356	338
Imports	102	99	103	95	93	98	105	119	116	146	122

EXHIBIT 10

UNITED STATES EXPORTS AND IMPORTS 1957-67
(Chemicals)

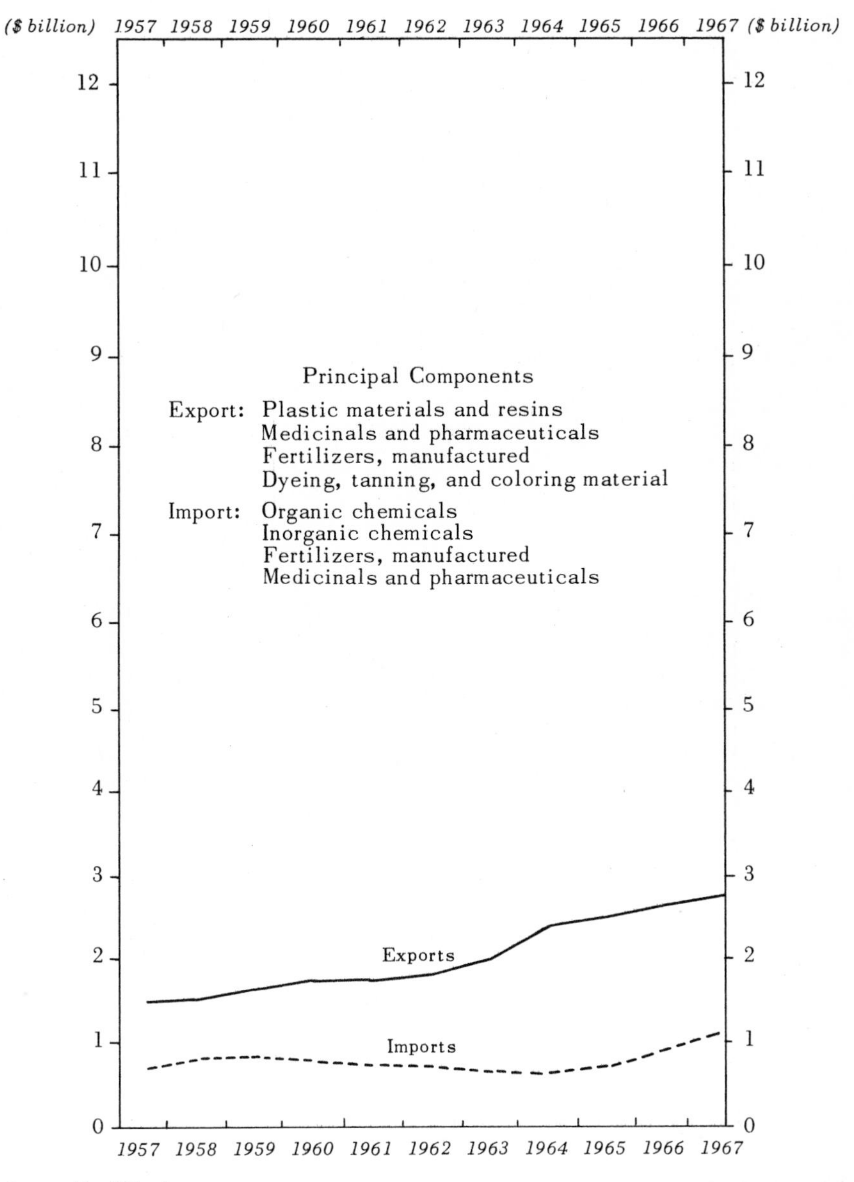

Data: ($ million)

1957	1958	1959	1960	1961	1962	1963	1964	1965	1966	1967
1,476	1,425	1,558	1,776	1,789	1,876	2,009	2,364	2,402	2,675	2,803
668	800	874	821	738	772	715	702	769	957	963

EXHIBIT 12

UNITED STATES EXPORTS AND IMPORTS 1957-67
(Other manufactured goods)

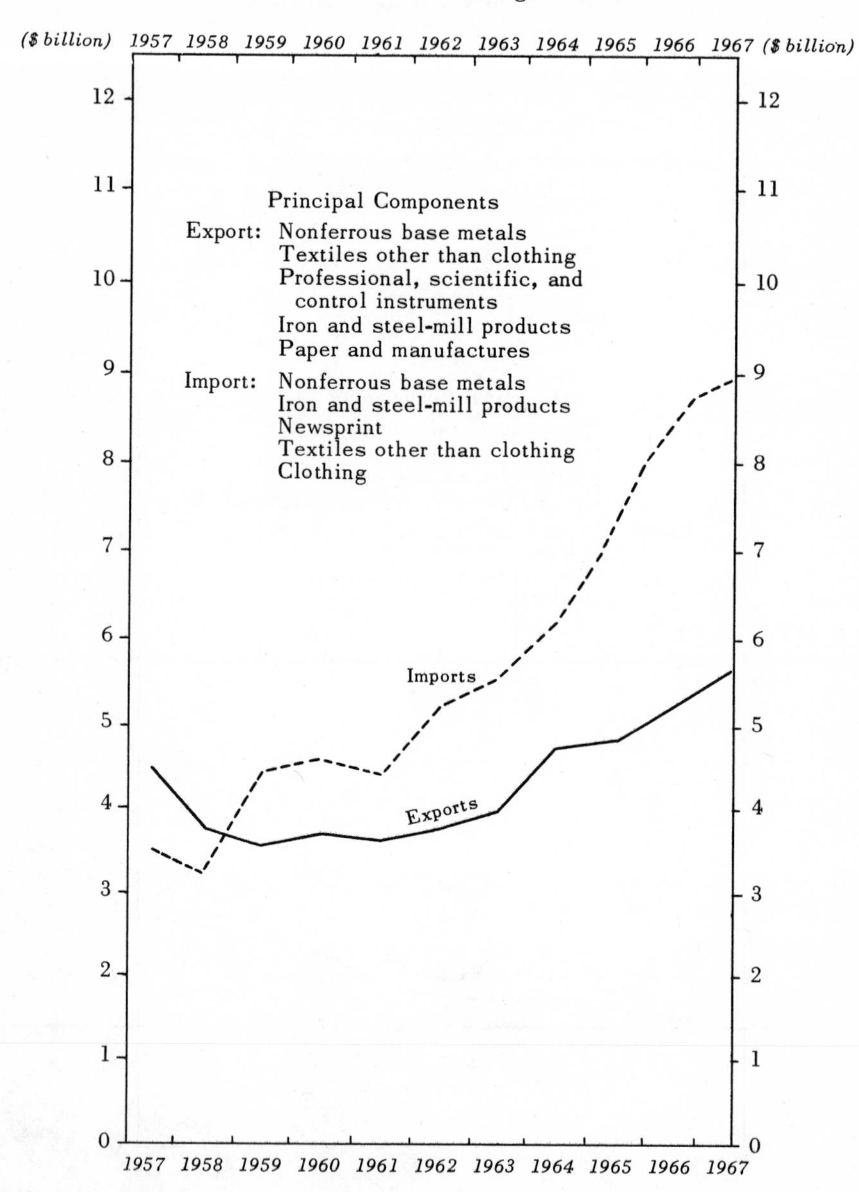

Data: ($ million)

4,349 3,731 3,537 3,791 3,646 3,753 4,007 4,655 4,839 5,276 5,376
3,542 3,240 4,401 4,559 4,421 5,180 5,532 6,178 7,521 8,636 8,963

EXHIBIT 11

UNITED STATES EXPORTS AND IMPORTS 1957-67
(Machinery and transport equipment)

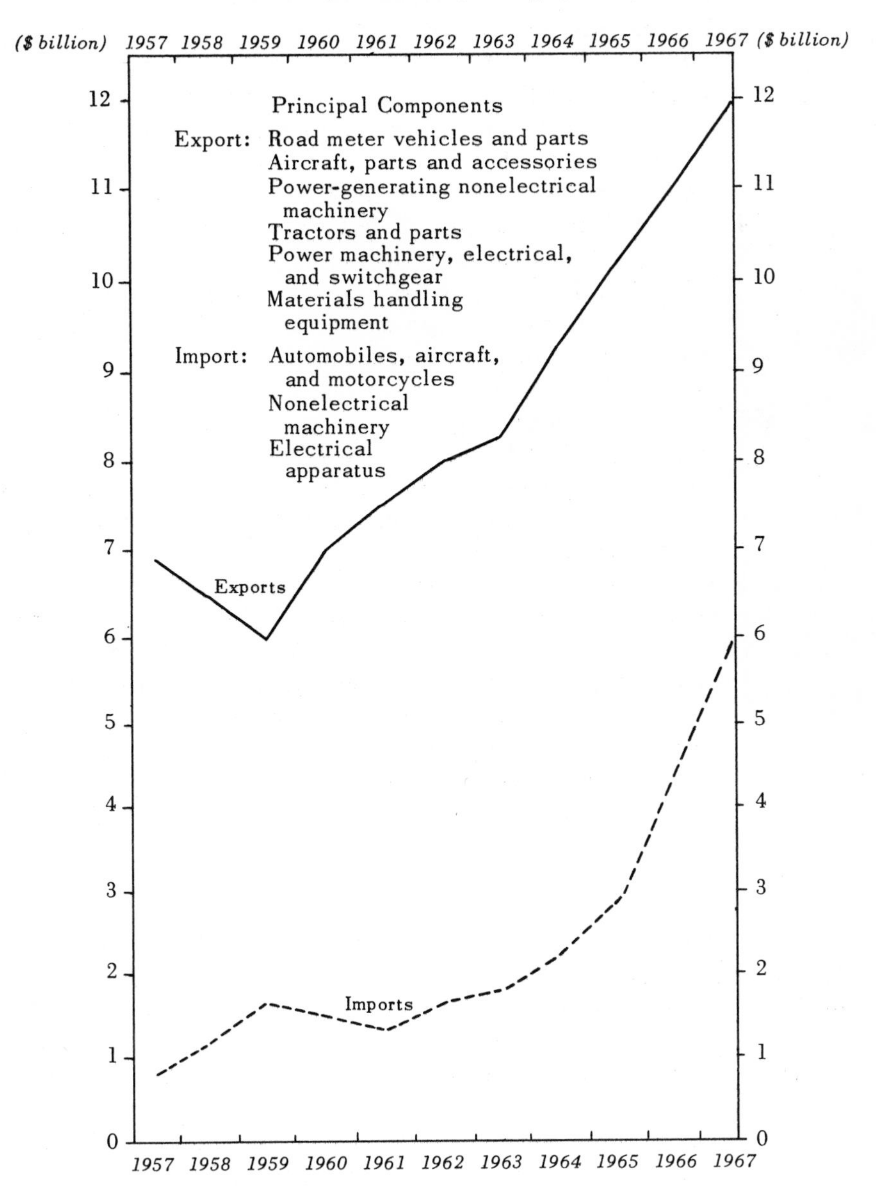

Data: ($ million)

6,869 6,390 6,076 6,992 7,313 8,026 8,243 9,369 10,147 11,155 12,573
862 1,150 1,630 1,467 1,364 1,674 1,819 2,216 2,948 4,823 5,791

live animals, in beverages and tobacco, in crude materials (except fuel), and in mineral fuels and related materials.

3. In other groupings, natural and comparative advantage and resultant specialization are more evident. For example, exports normally exceed imports of beverages and tobacco, of animal and vegetable oils and fats, of chemicals, and of machinery and transport equipment; while imports usually exceed exports of mineral fuels and of other manufactured goods.
4. The structure of foreign trade by SITC sectional aggregates remains relatively constant, judged by the result of the past ten years. That is, the relative position of export and import interest appears to remain fairly constant. In all of the groupings except two, the excess of exports or of imports was consistent year by year.
5. The most noticeable growth in the past decade in U.S. exports was in food and live animals (over $1 billion), in chemicals (about $1 billion), in machinery and transport equipment (about $4 billion, half of which occurred in the last year), and in other manufactured goods (some $5 billion).
6. One of the most outstanding changes in the entire picture over the past decade has been the increase of some $5 billion in imports of other manufactured goods (see Exhibit 12). In detail, this is traceable primarily to a greatly expanded volume of imports of iron and steel mill products (up about $1 billion); of nonferrous base metals (notably copper, aluminum, and nickel); of textiles other than clothing; of musical instruments and reproducers; and of toys, games, and sporting goods.

U.S. IMPORTANCE IN THE FOREIGN TRADE OF OTHER COUNTRIES

It has already been brought out that the United States is the largest foreign trader in the world, both as an exporter and as an importer, as measured by the dollar value of such trade. Therefore, it is an important market for their products to many exporters. This reliance on the part of others is reflected in Exhibit 13, which shows the proportion of exports of several selected countries which is sold to the United States.

Nine of the countries shown (see Exhibit 13) earn about a third of their foreign exchange from exports through sales to the United States, and three of these countries rather consistently send over half of their total exports to the United States. About 21 countries send over 5 percent of their total exports to the American economy. When it is realized that profit is made on

EXHIBIT 13

EXPORTS TO THE UNITED STATES AS A PERCENT OF TOTAL EXPORTS OF SELECTED COUNTRIES, 1966

50 percent or more:	Canada, Mexico, Panama
40-50 percent:	Colombia, Peru, Philippines
30-40 percent:	Brazil, Japan, Venezuela
20-30 percent:	Chile, Hong Kong
10-20 percent:	Australia, India, Israel, Nigeria, Pakistan, South Africa, Spain, Switzerland, Turkey, United Kingdom
1-5 percent:	Argentina, Belgium-Luxembourg, Denmark, France, West Germany, Italy, Netherlands, Norway, Sweden, Yugoslavia.

Note: The source of Exhibits 13-15 is as follows: *Overseas Business Reports* 67-43, U.S. Department of Commerce, Washington, D.C., 1967.

EXHIBIT 14

IMPORTS FROM THE UNITED STATES AS A PERCENT OF TOTAL IMPORTS OF SELECTED COUNTRIES, 1966

50 percent or more:	Canada, Mexico, Venezuela
40-50 percent:	Colombia, Panama
30-40 percent:	Brazil, Chile, India, Pakistan, Peru, Philippines
20-30 percent:	Argentina, Australia, Congo (Kinshasa), Israel, Japan, Turkey
10-20 percent:	France, Germany, Hong Kong, Italy, Netherlands, Nigeria, South Africa, Spain, United Kingdom, Yugoslavia
5-10 percent:	Belgium-Luxembourg, Denmark, Norway, Sweden, Switzerland

EXHIBIT 15

RELATIVE STANDING OF FOREIGN COUNTRIES AND AREAS AS MARKETS FOR U.S. EXPORTS AND SOUCES OF U.S. IMPORTS

(In percentages of U.S. total exports and imports, 1966)

Country or Area	*Percent of Exports*		*Percent of Imports*	
Canada		21.9		23.9
Central American Common Market		1.9		1.2
Latin American Free Trade Association		11.4		13.3
Argentina	.8		.5	
Brazil	1.9		2.3	
Chile	.8		.9	
Colombia	.9		.9	
Mexico	3.8		2.9	
Peru	1.0		1.2	
Venezuela	2.4		3.9	
Jamaica		*		.5
Netherlands Antilles		*		1.2
Trinidad and Tobago		*		.6
European Economic Community		18.1		16.1
Belgium-Luxembourg	2.3		2.2	
France	3.3		2.7	
Germany	5.5		7.0	
Italy	3.0		2.9	
Netherlands	4.0		1.2	
European Free Trade Association		9.8		11.5
Denmark	.6		.8	
Sweden	1.1		1.1	
Switzerland	1.3		1.5	
United Kingdom	5.7		7.0	
Greece		.6		*
Spain		1.8		.6
Turkey		.8		*
Yugoslavia		.5		*
Eastern Europe		.6		.7
Japan		7.8		11.6
Hong Kong		.7		1.6
India		3.0		1.3
Indonesia		*		.7
Malaysia and Singapore		*		.7
Pakistan		.8		*
Philippines		1.1		1.5
Australia		2.2		1.7
New Zealand and Western Samoa		.5		.7
South Africa		1.3		1.0
Iran		.7		*
Israel		.7		*
Lebanon		.5		*
United Arab Republic		.6		*
Korea		1.1		*
Taiwan		.7		*
South Vietnam		1.0		*

* Less than .5 percent.

the last 5 or 10 percent of sales rather than on the first, the significance of the United States as a trading partner is evident. And even without reference to profit, the foreign exchange earned by sales to the United States is a sizable part of that coming into possession of many countries. This explains in large part their interest in having the United States follow stable economic policies, because of the effect of economic activity on the level of imports.

Not only is the United States a major factor in the export trade of many countries, it is also important in their import trade. As shown in Exhibit 14, 11 countries obtain about a third or more of their imports from the United States; and in 3, all situated in relative proximity to the United States, the import markets are over half supplied by U.S. production. Since these figures are based on import statistics of the several countries, there is no differentiation as between straight commercial purchases and those that are financed by the U.S. Government, such as under Public Law 480. But the imports, or most of them, must eventually be paid, too, so the opportunity for these countries to earn dollars or other convertible exchange and the need or desire for viable credit terms to them are legitimate concerns of the United States in its own self-interest.

Looking at the relationship of trade with other countries from the viewpoint of the United States, one finds that there is far less concentrated dependence by the United States on any single country or even on regional groupings. This holds true either as a market for exports or a source of supply. The leading trading partners, in terms of percentages of U.S. exports to and imports from them in 1966, were as shown in Exhibit 15. The exhibit includes all countries which took as much as one-half of 1 percent of our exports or provided as much as one-half of 1 percent of our imports.

The tabulation brings out that only one country, Canada, takes as much as 10 percent of our exports and only three others, Japan, Germany, and the United Kingdom, take as much as 5 percent. Furthermore, only two countries, Canada and Japan, provide as much as 10 percent of our imports, and two others, United Kingdom and Germany, provide as much as 5 percent. Finally, one sees that after Canada the next most important market relationships are with the European Common Market and that the Latin American Free Trade Association (LAFTA) and the European Free Trade Association (EFTA) are about equal in position in U.S. foreign trade, each being about half as important as Canada is and about equal to Japan as a source of U.S. imports.

Chapter II

Foreign Investments

With the exception of trade in merchandise, which accounts for the largest segment of the balance of payments, in no area of international economic transactions are there more interest and significance than in international investment. In fact, private capital transactions and income on foreign investments constitute the second most important segment of the summary of international transactions of the United States.

The urgency of our imbalance of payments in the 1960's and strictures against certain foreign investments focused major attention on such investments. While both voluntary and mandatory steps pertaining to foreign investment were employed to redress the unfavorable balance of payments picture, there also evolved helpful analyses and presentations concerning the relationship between investments and exports of merchandise. In part this can be attributed to the availability of more complete statistics on such investments, and certainly public discussion led to a better understanding of this relationship and perhaps to less pressure for a compulsory cutback on investments across the board. Much of what was done was selective.

Composition of investments. Foreign investments, from the broader and liberal balance of payments viewpoint of *claims on* or *liabilities to foreigners,* are of varied types—stocks, bonds, physical property, bank balances, accounts and notes receivable, short-term investments (acceptances and commercial paper), and drafts in the process of collection. But in assessing the country's total foreign investment position, one must recognize that not all foreign investments (or liabilities) are private. Government also owns a handsome portfolio of claims on foreigners, these being direct government-to-government advances, claims on foreign debtors owned by the Export-Import Bank, foreign currencies acquired under special programs, such as Public Law 480, subscriptions to international institutions, such as the International Monetary Fund and the International Bank for Reconstruction and Development, and foreign currency holdings acquired by the Treasury from other operations conducted for it by the Federal Reserve Bank of New York.

Still another category of what may be called foreign investments—that is, claims on foreigners—should include holdings of foreign currencies by Federal Reserve Banks, acquired primarily in foreign exchange market support operations and changing daily. In contrast are liabilities due foreign monetary authorities by Federal Reserve Banks.

Direct vs. portfolio investments. Private foreign investments, which are blamed by some for at least part of the balance of payments deficit, fall into two main categories—direct and portfolio. For statistical purposes, the Department of Commerce defines "direct" investments as those made for the purpose of control in some effective degree over some foreign operation. Its line of demarcation for some time was that 25 percent of equity ownership constitutes a direct investment. However, beginning in the late 1950's, the extent of participation needed to qualify as "direct" was set at 10 percent, which is consistent with minimum ownership required in order to be able to claim income tax credits under internal revenue laws. A lesser percentage of ownership or the holding of evidences of debt would, on the other hand, be considered as "portfolio" investments.

Why foreign investments are made. The motives out of which the several types of foreign investment spring are several. First, and as a general statement, is the desire on the part of individuals for greater safety or greater income. Second, there is the element of speculation and arbitrage operations. And third, a substantial part of foreign investments, as defined in the fuller sense, consists of working funds which arise from or facilitate the conduct of business. These are not "deliberate" investments, so they can hardly be said to have a motive; they are, rather, the result of other actions or decisions.

As to direct investment by industry, the major impelling forces seem to be: (1) intensive cultivation of a foreign market, which can best be done by an arrangement which requires investment and direct, active control; (2) manufacturing abroad in order to get into a country or an area under its tariff or other protective wall (automobiles, pharmaceuticals, food), or because of lower costs; and (3) to develop or protect a source of raw materials (rubber, copper, oil).

Foreign investments, also being made by governments, may be principally political or military in motive. Economic considerations would appear to be more in the nature of means to an end. And, of course, the foreign currencies obtained in the process of market support are acquired with a motive all their own.

How foreign investments are made. Property abroad can be acquired in several ways. The first method is by cash purchase—of minority interest in a foreign company, of half interest, of majority interest, or of full ownership. Or payment may be made in kind—by the provision of machinery or equipment or services, for varying degrees of ownership. As in domestic finance, investment interest may be increased by the retention of earnings. Another method of acquiring a foreign investment, at least in conformity with definition, is by making loans or other credit advances abroad. These include the normal day-to-day financing of ordinary business. And still another is by building up equity interest by the process of not withdrawing royalties or fees deriving from continued use of industrial property rights or of services.

Impact on foreign exchange. In considering the impact of foreign investment on foreign exchange, there are several channels by which such an impact can be felt. First, however, one must look on the relationship between investment and foreign exchange in point of time: (1) at the time of making the initial investment; (2) the continued servicing of the investment; (3) transactions, by sale or purchase, in the investment or in part of it; and (4) liquidation of the investment, if that should occur out of necessity or voluntarily.

If the investment is an outright cash purchase, such as buying into an established foreign business with payment in cash, the impact would be a demand for foreign currency on the part of the American buyer or the sale of the dollars newly acquired by the foreign business—that is, unless one American firm bought from another. The continued servicing of the investment, meaning the payment of dividends, interest, royalties, or fees, creates a demand for dollars or, alternatively, for the sale of the foreign currency by the American recipient thereof, unless it is used for additional investment by him or otherwise spent abroad. The Department of Commerce reports that income (interest and dividends) on U.S. direct investments abroad amounted in 1966 to $4,045 million, and that royalties and fees, excluding film rentals abroad, received by U.S. interests on their direct investments amounted to $1,045 million.[1] Of the latter figure, $659 million was from manufacturing industries.

Transactions in securities. Transactions in securities have a more direct and immediate impact on the foreign exchange market than do transactions in merchandise for the simple reason that they are normally sold for cash rather than on credit terms, and certainly not on medium- or long-term

[1] *Survey of Current Business,* U.S. Department of Commerce, Washington, D.C., September 1967, pp. 22, 49.

credit. The volume of international transactions in securities is more important in its impact on foreign exchange (and the balance of payments) than appears to be generally appreciated. For example, in several recent years sales to foreigners of securities (American corporate bonds and stocks, foreign bonds and stocks, and U.S. Government securities) amounted to around 25 to 30 percent of our exports of merchandise (see Exhibit 16), and purchases of securities from foreigners were frequently as much as 35 to 45 percent of our imports of merchandise (see Exhibit 17).

Relation of investments to U.S. exports. The public attention raised by the balance of payments deficit in 1962 and 1963 resulted in a better under-

EXHIBIT 16

SALES OF SECURITIES TO FOREIGNERS, AS A PERCENTAGE OF EXPORTS OF MERCHANDISE

Year	*Domestic Corporate and other Stocks and Bonds*	*Foreign Stocks and Bonds*	*U. S. Government Securities*	*Total of Securities*
1950	8	8	12	27
1951	6	5	5	16
1952	6	5	4	14
1953	5	5	4	15
1954	9	7	5	23
1955	12	9	9	30
1956	10	7	5	22
1957	8	6	3	17
1958	10	8	7	25
1959	15	9	7	31
1960	12	7	9	27
1961	16	7	8	31
1962	12	8	8	29
1963	13	7	8	28
1964	14	6	4	24
1965	17	8	4	28
1966	22	9	2	33

Source for Exhibits 16 and 17: Calculated from data in *Treasury Bulletin*, December, 1963, January 1966, and April 1967, and in *Overseas Business Reports* for applicable years.

EXHIBIT 17

PURCHASES OF SECURITIES FROM FOREIGNERS, AS A PERCENT OF IMPORTS OF MERCHANDISE

Year	*Domestic Corporate and other Stocks and Bonds*	*Foreign Stocks and Bonds*	*U. S. Government Securities*	*Total of Securities*
1950	9	10	3	22
1951	7	11	12	30
1952	8	9	2	19
1953	7	9	7	24
1954	12	15	8	35
1955	15	12	7	35
1956	13	15	8	36
1957	11	16	6	32
1958	14	21	9	44
1959	14	15	4	33
1960	15	14	11	40
1961	22	15	8	45
1962	15	17	15	48
1963	16	16	7	39
1964	20	13	8	41
1965	22	14	5	42
1966	22	13	5	41

standing of the interplay between foreign direct investment and American exports. Public interest was facilitated by a series of special studies by experts in the Department of Commerce, which had developed primary statistical data for the purpose.

In one of these studies, "Financing and Sales of Foreign Affiliates of United States Firms,"[2] it was brought out that a relatively small part of the output of these affiliates enters international trade among foreign countries or between the host countries and the United States. In 1964, for example, total sales of foreign manufacturing affiliates were $37.3 billion, of which $30.6 billion was local to the country in which situated. Some $1.6 billion

[2] *Ibid.*, November 1965.

was exported by these affiliates to the United States, and a little over $5 billion was exported to other countries.

Considerable testimony was offered by business spokesmen before Congressional committees as to the importance of foreign manufacturing affiliates to American exports. And the Department of Commerce began to collect and publish more specific data and analyses on the subject. One study provided statistical evidence that exports to affiliates are a major element in total U.S. exports. They were 25 percent of all U.S. exports in 1964, as compared with 24 percent in 1962 and 1963. In the category of nonagricultural exports, the proportion taken by foreign affiliates was even higher—one-third of the total in 1964.[3]

It is thus evident that the distribution facilities set up to dispose of goods manufactured abroad must also be a very useful facility in disposing of certain U.S. manufactures that might not otherwise be exported. Hence the feeling on the part of some that, rather than adopting policies that lead to a cutback or a slowdown in such investments, government policy should be to encourage them, or at least not discourage them, because of their contribution to expanded exports in general.

ASSISTANCE TO PRIVATE INVESTORS

While private foreign investments by U.S. interests clearly benefit the overall export and foreign trade position of the United States, they also serve another important overall foreign policy objective. That is the provision of meaningful assistance in the economic development of less-developed friendly countries. Accordingly, the U.S. posture has been to encourage actively not only our exports but also the undertaking of certain private investments in less-developed friendly countries. This is done by finding and publicizing investment opportunities, by offering guarantees or insurance against certain risks involved in foreign investment, and, occasionally, by direct financial assistance.

The function of finding and publicizing investment and licensing opportunities is performed in all foreign countries, regardless of their stage of economic development. In addition, in the less-developed countries, part of the cost of surveys to determine the feasibility of an investment may be covered by the Agency for International Development (AID), if prior arrangements for doing so have been made. In appropriate cases AID will agree to cover half the cost of a feasibility study if the potential investor who makes

[3] *Ibid.*, December 1965, p. 12.

the survey decides not to invest. In that case the survey becomes the property of AID and is available to other potential investors.

Direct financial assistance, as offered by the U.S. Government to private American foreign investors, normally takes the form of guarantees or of insurance against certain risks involved in private foreign investment. However, provision is also made for direct loans to American investors in projects deemed desirable when funds are not available elsewhere—that is, practically as a source of last resort.

Assistance to these foreign investment activities is provided by the U.S. Government principally through AID and the Export-Import Bank. A third source of direct assistance is found in the Commodity Credit Corporation, which sells commodities on credit terms of up to three years to American exporters, who, in turn, are then more easily able to extend credit to foreign buyers and thereby build up U.S. exports and foreign credit claims.

Agency for International Development (AID). This agency is the successor of a line of agencies designed to assist financially and technologically in the economic recovery of other countries—originally for reconstruction following the war and more recently for economic development of underdeveloped countries. The foreign aid program as now known began with the Marshall Plan, when the Economic Cooperation Administration (ECA) was established to assist in the economic recovery of Europe.

The principal manner in which AID assists the private American investor is through its investment guaranty program, which affords protection against certain political and business risks. These risks, against which protection is deemed desirable, are:

- Inability to convert into dollars the foreign currency received as earnings or as return of principal.
- Confiscation or expropriation.
- War, revolution, or insurrection.

The risks enumerated are considered political in nature, and guaranties against them, or at least some of them, are available in over 75 countries under what is known as specific risk coverage. Under the foregoing, the risk of devaluation is not included. Before guaranties can be issued, the foreign government must have signed an agreement with the U.S. Government concerning procedures and relations between the two governments for administration of the program; for if the U.S. Government pays the insured, it then takes up a claim against the foreign government. Guaranties against war risks (including revolution and insurrection) are available in almost 70 countries. Guaranties are limited to new investments, including expansion or modernization of existing investments, and the foreign country must approve the individual investment before AID will issue its guaranty. The investor may apply for blanket or partial protection in each case.

In certain priority investment situations, AID began to offer, in 1961, insurance coverage under an "extended risk guaranty program," covering all risks listed under the specific risk program plus others, such as currency devaluation and normal business risks, but excluding risks such as fraud and misconduct of the investor and those risks, such as fire and theft, for which commercial insurance is available. This program is mainly designed to attract long-term credit from U.S. institutional lenders to help finance private projects.[4]

Aside from its investment guaranty programs, AID considers requests for dollar loans to private American enterprise for investment abroad, but in order to obtain the funds, the applicant must show the nonavailability of financing from private sources on reasonable terms.

The Export-Import Bank (Eximbank). As the original U.S. agency engaging in the granting of direct financial assistance specifically for foreign trade, the bank is charged, as a primary responsibility, with assisting in the expansion of U.S. exports. An aftereffect of sales on credit, as indicated earlier, is reflected in the foreign investment position of the United States. It is from this point of view that current attention is focused on the bank's private foreign investment assistance.

Eximbank loans are made primarily to foreign entities (government or private) for a long term, either as project loans or to finance the purchase of capital equipment, or they may take the form of short- and medium-term exporter and commodity credits. Loans made by the Eximbank appear as assets in the international investment position of the United States and thereby increase our creditor position (or reduce our net debtor position). There is no equity financing by the Eximbank.

Long-term project loans constitute the principal type of foreign investment in which the Export-Import Bank participates. Loans of this type are made for periods of from 5 to 20 years and are made only when there is reasonable prospect of repayment.

Short- and medium-term exporter and commodity credits by the Eximbank have become less important in total in recent years as a program was developed to encourage the credits being advanced by private commercial banks under Eximbank guaranties or through purchase of the underlying paper from Eximbank by commercial banks, and more recently through di-

[4] *World Business,* Chase Manhattan Bank, New York, July 1966, pp. 5–6.

rect loans to commercial banks to encourage their carrying of medium-term export credits.

As of June 1967, as shown in its annual report to Congress, the bank since its inception had authorized credits of $18,977 million, worldwide. Of this amount, $10,496 million had been disbursed or was still active and $8,481 million had been repaid or had expired. It is thus evident that this source of direct long-term credit is significant not only in the U.S. export picture, but also in the overall foreign investment position of the United States.

FOREIGN ATTITUDES TOWARD U.S. DIRECT INVESTMENTS

Despite the various government programs to stimulate private foreign investment by U.S. interests, one would be less than practical were he to assume that the environment for international investment by U.S. interests is one of a crying desire abroad for American money and know-how. This is certainly so where private investment finds it relatively unattractive and too risky to go in unprotected or unassisted. But there are many cases, among both developed and less-developed countries, in which American investment is welcome only on a selective and controlled basis.

In fact, investment by foreigners in most countries is subject to government approval; the free international mobility of capital and manpower and their free employment simply do not exist. Moreover, the convertibility in currencies achieved in the postwar period is only on current account; capital movements remain under control by national authorities. Furthermore, many countries operate their economies under more or less of an economic plan. There may be a vague or specific blueprint; there probably are sectors of the economy or sections of the country that, in the eyes of the national government, need protection or expansion. Hence one can well understand the suspicions and sometimes hostile attitudes found abroad concerning U.S. direct investments.

An informal survey of European businessmen, concerning their attitudes toward direct U.S. investments in their countries, conducted in 1965 by the Chamber of Commerce of the United States, brought out both positive and negative feelings. These professional attitudes reflected in certain instances, and certainly influenced, some of the government attitudes that had to be faced by American business in establishing itself abroad. On the positive side there was widespread desire for American capital and technology, but in several cases this was tempered with the desire for more participation in management, more joint ventures, and even majority control—especially in certain sensitive industries—and more cooperation, coordination, and contact between local and U.S. businessmen. On the negative, or critical, side many observations were made reflecting roots which are political, psychological, and emotional. Among such criticisms, annoyances, and fears (actual or potential) were the following:

- American subsidiaries did not employ enough qualified host country nationals in management of the company.
- American firms did not understand or did not adequately study and respect local laws, customs, and regulations, especially in the areas of employee relations and social legislation.
- U.S. antitrust attitudes and laws were different from those to which the Europeans had been accustomed.
- Subsidiaries often lacked authority, and tight home-office (U.S.) control was apt to be insensitive to purely local conditions abroad.
- Some U.S. firms engaged in overbidding for personnel, thus driving up wages and costs for national companies.
- U.S. firms were insufficiently sensitive to national economic planning. Their control from abroad and access to funds and other assistance from abroad made it less necessary for them than for purely national companies to conform to such planning.
- Higher-paid U.S. managers were working side by side with lower-paid host country managers.
- American firms, because of size and resources available, were tending to penetrate dangerously and/or to dominate certain industries, some of key importance, such as automobiles, aircraft, computers, pharmaceuticals, and others of significance to national defense.
- Centers of decision and research were passing out of national control and into American hands.
- U.S. official policies and attitudes concerning East-West trade differed from those of other countries, and U.S. subsidiaries abroad were thereby constrained in developing this business, considered desirable for its economy by the host country in which the subsidiary was located.

Generalizing from these expressions of individual attitudes, which originated in seven European countries, may give one an overly pessimistic view of foreign attitudes toward U.S. investments. But similar observations have emanated from Canada, Japan, and some Latin American countries, many of which desire to attract American capital and know-how, but desire just as much to retain a strong national flavor in the control, orientation, and effort of their economies.

PRINCIPAL INVESTING NATIONS

One of the gaps in our overall economic intelligence is lack of information concerning the foreign investment positions of the major countries of the world. Data are available on merchandise transactions and on certain other international exchanges, but only a few countries appear to have collected or published data on their overall international investment positions.

Among the countries that publish foreign investment statements are the United States, the United Kingdom, Canada, Denmark, and Norway. Other countries, such as India and South Africa, have conducted censuses of this nature; and still others, such as Venezuela and Mexico, compile data on certain aspects of their international investment positions. Otherwise, it is known that France, Germany, Japan, the Netherlands, Belgium, and Switzerland are significant forces in the overall international investment world.

Chapter III

Overall Trading and Investment Positions of the United States

In the preceding chapters we have concerned ourselves with selected dimensions of the universe of international business. This also demonstrated the significance of the United States as a trading nation and gave some reference to our importance in the international economic relations of other individual countries. This chapter will now deal with U.S. transactions with the rest of the world from the viewpoint of "balance" and of relationship with certain aspects of the domestic economy.

The standard tools or devices for doing so are: (1) a statistical presentation known as the balance of payments (sometimes referred to as Summary of International Transactions), and (2) a second presentation generally titled "The International Investment Position of the United States." In accounting terminology, the balance of payments is somewhat akin to an operating, or profit and loss, statement, in that it purports to reflect the summation of various transactions or net changes in certain accounts during a given period of time. The international investment position presentation is more closely comparable to a balance sheet, in that it purports to reflect a position as of a given date.

THE BALANCE OF PAYMENTS

The balance of payments is a summation of our international transactions (aggregates or net changes) in a given time period, arranged in "debit" and "credit" order, or perhaps listed as "receipts" and "payments." Its most important practical function is to indicate how we got where we are; what changes took place in our international accounts; why, economically but not psychologically, changes in gold or monetary reserves took place, or at least what some of the major international economic activity was that accounted for or influenced a change in our international economic position. In the case of the United States, the balance of payments is drawn up quarterly and annually; in other countries this is generally less frequent—more likely only annually. Both the quarterly and the annual statements become available some three months after closing date, and since they incorporate transactions that took place perhaps 6 to 15 months earlier, they constitute a report quite some time after the fact.

As indicated earlier, the balance of payments brings into one picture a conglomeration of aggregate transactions in goods and services plus net changes in capital and investment accounts. Yet it does not provide an inventory position, nor does it give any indication of our liquidity position as of a closing date, but it does show changes in the position during the period covered.

One sometimes hears that the balance of payments statement is comparable to a double-entry system of accounting for our international economic transactions, but this is not literally correct. A double-entry bookkeeping system means that two entries, a debit and a credit, are made from the same basic document. This is not the case in the construction of a balance of payments, as will be seen later.

Order of presentation. As can be seen by reference to a standard presentation,[1] the major components of the balance of payments are:

- Exports and imports of goods and services.
- Unilateral transfers.
- Transactions in U.S. private capital and investments.
- Transactions in U.S. Government assets, excluding official reserve assets.
- Transactions in U.S. official reserve assets.

[1] See, for example, *Survey of Current Business,* U.S. Department of Commerce, Washington, D.C., March 1967.

- Transactions in foreign assets in the United States.
- Errors and omissions.

Most of these include one or more subdivisions providing detail or type. In the usual accompanying analysis, changes occurring during the period are explained, and the accounts may be rearranged or balanced out in order to arrive at an approximate accounting for and explanation of changes in monetary reserve assets, which include gold, convertible currencies, and the U.S. gold tranche position in the International Monetary Fund.

The relative net importance of the principal types of transactions making up the overall current picture (not capital movements) is indicated by Exhibit 18.

EXHIBIT 18

RELATIVE STATUS OF MAJOR U.S. INTERNATIONAL CURRENT TRANSACTIONS
(Figures in $ million)

Year	*Merchandise*	*Transportation*	*Travel*	*Miscellaneous Services**	*Income on Investments*
1960	+4,736**	–301	– 869	+ 677	+2,321
1961	+5,416	–100	– 862	+ 722	+2,962
1962	+4,442	–190	–1,022	+ 895	+3,326
1963	+4,993	–232	–1,136	+1,025	+3,273
1964	+6,581	–195	–1,086	+1,100	+3,858
1965	+4,788	–276	–1,188	+1,415	+4,255
1966	+3,673	–318	–1,306	+1,556	+4,312
1967	+3,483	–264	–1,529	+1,648	+4,506

* Includes fees and royalties from direct investments.
** "Plus" signifies net export; "minus" signifies net import.

Source: Data for 1960-64, *Statistical Abstract of the United States*, U. S. Department of Commerce, Washington, D. C., 1965, p. 866; for 1965 and 1966, *Survey of Current Business*, U. S. Department of Commerce, Washington, D. C., March 1967, p. 19; for 1967, *Survey of Current Business*, March 1968, p. 23.

By far the largest item in the broad category of current transactions is trade in merchandise. Of the total of current transactions (gross, not net), merchandise accounts for about two-thirds, whether export or import. Our second largest "export" on current account is the use of American capital abroad, reported as "Income on Investments." This activity yielded about 13 percent of the total of exports in 1966. After merchandise, our second and third largest imports, excluding military expenditures, are normally transportation and travel. Transportation services purchased from foreigners accounted for almost 8 percent of imports of all goods and services in 1966, while expenditures on travel were 7 percent.

Interpretation of selected accounts. In order to comprehend more fully the usual balance of payment presentation, or to understand the changes reflected therein, the following comments on selected accounts will suggest the need for a cautious acceptance of the simple statistical figures:

- Merchandise, adjusted. As just indicated, this item represents about two-thirds of current "receipts" and "payments." But it is not a completely accurate indication of actual receipt of payment. First of all one must consider the origin of the data, and then the fact that the figures have been adjusted. The primary sources of data are the Shippers Export Declaration and the Import Entry, each of which prescribes guidelines intended to show primarily the value of goods physically crossing the frontier. On these documents there is no place to show whether the goods were paid for in advance or will ever be paid for, or on what terms. Valuation procedures are also prescribed, so the valuation used does not necessarily represent invoice amounts. In the balance of payments concept, merchandise trade is intended to represent all movable goods which are sold, given away, or otherwise transferred to foreign ownership, or vice versa. Therefore, adjustments must be made in the aggregates derived from the basic documents.

  Exports of merchandise normally exceed imports. This has been U.S. experience for many years. But the difference is somewhat less real than appears. U.S. exports and imports are both valued at the port of exportation. But United Nations practice, as used by most countries, values imports at the port of importation (cost, insurance, and freight), so in this sense the United States undervalues its imports.
- Transportation. This is a rather important type of international transaction, running about 7 percent of "receipts" and 8 to 9 percent of "payments." But payments normally exceed receipts in amount. The content of this account is freight (ocean, Great Lakes, and air), passenger fares, port expenditures by vessels, and railway operations on in-transit freight.
- Travel. This account is normally larger as an import than as an

export—that is, Americans traveling abroad spend more than foreigners visiting the United States. And it is rather sizable, being about 7 to 8 percent of imports and 3 percent of exports. Over $2 billion of "imports" of this type were reported in recent years, with a net deficit of well over $1 billion.

- Income on investments. The nature of this account is primarily one of export rather than import, and it is growing. It represents payment by foreigners for the use of American capital, largely private. This means, moreover, a net demand by foreigners for dollars with which to meet their obligations.
- U.S. and foreign capital. These accounts reflect the substantial outflow of both private and Government capital in the postwar period, and especially since 1957. The figures for these accounts in the balance of payments represent *net* changes between two reporting dates; they are therefore not aggregates or accumulations, and the transactions over the period could have been substantial and volatile, with very serious impact on both exchange rates and monetary reserves.

Interrelationship between selected accounts. In the ordinary course of business, goods are not paid for on the day they are exported or imported. Final payment for exports, for example, may be days, weeks, or even months late. Normal financial procedure gives rise to a draft on the foreign buyer or his bank which, if unpaid at the closing date of the balance of payments period, appears then as an increase in claims on foreigners, or a net capital outflow. If more goods are sold on credit, or if the same volume is sold on more liberal credit terms, and the drafts are still in process of collection, the larger will be the reported short-term capital outflow.

Another important interrelationship between selected accounts is that pertaining to merchandise exports and direct investments. Not only are capital goods sent abroad for use in an investment reported as exports of merchandise, but from a fourth to a third of total exports are consigned to affiliates abroad at American firms.

Uses of balance of payments. With all the shortcomings indicated above, one may wonder whether such a presentation is worth the cost. Why do we need it? How may it be used?

First of all, the balance of payments is a useful instrument for policy guidance. Close study of the report over time may point up evolving trouble spots so that anticipatory remedies may be employed by managers of the economy. The relationships between elements of the statement help to explain what happened—not necessarily why, but what. From another view, the presentation is, in effect, an effort to identify the economic pressures that brought about a change in holdings of gold and monetary reserves.

The balance of payments appears not to be of such practical use to private citizens except perhaps as an explanation of what happened to bring about large changes in exchange rates and monetary reserves or why certain Government policies were undertaken or now appear justified. It does contribute to a better understanding of economic forces and pressures and trends and is therefore a useful reference for bank and corporate policies over the long pull.

INTERNATIONAL INVESTMENT POSITION OF THE UNITED STATES

The balance of payments, as just indicated, gives no evidence of standing at the end of a period, or as of a given date. For this, one must look to the second major presentation showing the international investment position of the United States, which is usually published annually in the *Survey of Current Business.*

This tabulation is a listing of American assets abroad and of foreign assets in the United States. It includes both private and governmental, and both long- and short-term, property and obligations. Throwing this all together into one statement does not mean, however, that the U.S. Government can take over or use the assets under present legislation; however, the Government can and does follow policies that amount to effective influencing, if not regulation, of such activities.

U.S. foreign investment activity, both ways, is very substantial, as shown by Exhibit 19. Perhaps the most striking feature of the overall investment position is that the values of U.S. assets and investments abroad and of foreign-owned assets and investments in the United States have more than tripled since 1950; and that the gross investment position of the United States is that of a "creditor" by some $52 billion. The main growth in U.S. investments abroad has been in private, direct investments; the main growth in foreign-owned investments in the United States has been in the form of short-term claims, although a significant increase is reported in foreigners' holdings of U.S. corporate stocks. Fortunately, the bulk of foreign short-term claims is held by central banks and governments. There is close intergovernmental cooperation on financial matters, so the risk of a "run" on the part of other governments—that is, large-scale demands for conversion of such claims into other foreign exchange than the dollar or into gold—is minimized.

Changes in the international investment position should logically take

EXHIBIT 19

INTERNATIONAL INVESTMENT POSITION OF THE UNITED STATES, 1950, 1963, AND 1966
(In billions of dollars)

	1950		*1963*		*1966*	
U. S. Assets and Investments Abroad:*						
Private		19		66		86
Long-term	17		58		75	
Direct	(12)		(41)		(55)	
Short-term	2		8		11	
U. S. Government credits and claims		13		22		26
Long-term	11		17		21	
Short-term	2		5		5	
Total		32		88		112
Foreign-owned Assets and Investments in United States						
Long-term		8		23		27
Direct	(3)		(8)		(9)	
Corporate stocks	(3)		(13)		(13)	
Bonds and other	(2)		(2)		(5)	
Short-term		10		29		33
Central banks and governments	n. a.		(19)		(18)	
Commercial banks	n. a.		(6)		(10)	
Other	n. a.		(4)		(5)	
Total		18		52		60
Net U. S. Creditor Position		14		36		52
*Gold stock not included in assets		22.8		15.6		13.2

Source: *Survey of Current Business*, U. S. Department of Commerce, Washington, D. C., September 1965, p. 32; September 1966, p. 40; September 1967, p. 40.

place only through transactions as summarized in the balance of payments. But the sheer volume of the work, different reporting dates, and definitions, and the fact that the reports are pieced together from a variety of sources, documents, and estimates, some of them adjusted, rather than being the result of a master set of books based on a double-entry bookkeeping system, make this impossible. Nevertheless, the reports, especially the one showing the international investment position, dramatically reflect a central problem of some years running. It is that the United States has been experiencing a cumulative deficit in its overall international accounts. The result is not only that we have lost large amounts of gold, as is indicated in the usual balance of payments statements, but that we are faced with substantial amounts of, and significant increases in, short-term liabilities convertible into gold, and other foreign-owned investments that could be liquidated on short notice. This is perhaps the central international economic problem of the 1960's.

ADJUSTMENTS IN INTERNATIONAL ECONOMIC RELATIONS

The problem of economic adjustments to keep the total of a nation's international purchases and sales in balance is many sided. The balance of payments covers all transactions—public and private, merchandise and investments, travel and services—all of the nation's economic transactions with the rest of the world. For the United States the problem's critical status is also not new. It dates at least from 1958 in sizable measure, although the trend began in the early 1950's.

One may wonder whether there ever is a solution to the situation illustrated by a balance of payments and a change in a nation's international investment position. Perhaps it would help to picture the totality of international economic transactions as a boat floating on water, subject to wind, waves, and tide. It (the international economic activity of each nation) must constantly adjust, or reconcile, to changing situations. In effect these situations reflect market reconciliations of international values and relationships, and the adjustment must be made by changes in domestic prices or economic activity in such areas as:

- Prices, themselves, including transportation.
- Interest rates and private capital movements (which must be free to move).
- Levels of income and employment.
- Exchange rates.

It appears that the best one can hope for in the sum total of international transactions is a reasonable equilibrium in the totality, so that *major* adjustments in the domestic economies will not be forced.

RESTRAINTS UNDER BALANCE OF PAYMENTS EMERGENCY

The United States has long followed a policy of free convertibility of the dollar into other foreign exchanges and no control over capital movements. However, in the early 1960's it was forced to take certain actions, short of direct and mandatory controls over capital movements, that would have the effect of mitigating the outflow of capital. This was done to defend the monetary reserves of the dollar.

The first of these measures was imposition of an interest equalization tax (Public Law 88–563) in mid-1963, one of whose objects was to bring about a dampening of foreign borrowing in the United States, which had increased to take advantage of lower interest rates here. The tax was imposed on the first-time acquisition by U.S. citizens of stock of a foreign issuer and of bonds of a foreign obligor. The tax on stock was 15 percent of its value. The tax on bonds was graduated and applied to issues having a period remaining to maturity of three years or more. It ranged from 2.75 percent of the value of the security for the shortest maturity (3 to 3½ years) to 15 percent for the longest (28½ years or more).

A number of exceptions to the measure's applicability were made by excluding from its coverage such items as direct investments, investments in less-developed countries, securities acquired from American owners who could meet specified qualifications, or new issues required for international monetary stability. It is under the latter authority that the President was able to make special arrangements regarding applicability of the tax to Canada and Japan.

The restraint on transactions in securities should be consistent with policies in general pertaining to the balance of payments deficit. There was, therefore, pressure for more fundamental, even if less direct, steps, a very important one being higher interest rates in the United States as an inducement to the employment of American-owned funds in the United States. Sizable volumes had gone abroad to take advantage of higher interest rates prevailing in foreign markets. Accordingly, a modest increase in the Federal Reserve discount rate was authorized at the time the equalization tax was first imposed. Some felt the increase was not adequate, but authorities felt the effect of much higher rates on the domestic economy at that time would have been too high a price to pay for a quick stemming of the outflow of funds.

However, the balance of payments deficit persisted and at times worsened. This led to a major ten-point message from President Johnson to the Congress in February 1965. The message announced or requested action pertaining to foreign investments, the program providing for or contemplating the following:

- Extension of the life of the interest equalization tax and broadening of its coverage to nonbank loans of from one to three years. Legislation was passed to this effect, extending the tax through

July 1967 (Public Law 89–243). Later it was extended to July 31, 1969 (Public Law 90–59).

- Application of the interest equalization tax to bank loans of one year or more.
- Assurance by Canada that its policies would attempt to curb excessive flows of funds to the Dominion. Transactions with Canada are not subject to the same constrictions as are those with Europe.
- Enrollment of the banking community in a major effort to limit its loans abroad. For this, the Federal Reserve established guidelines, the major one being the request to limit outstanding credits to foreigners to not more than 105 percent of the amounts outstanding at the end of 1964. Within this, banks were requested to give highest priority to the needs for export credits and then to loans to less-developed countries.
- Legislation exempting commercial banks from antitrust laws when they cooperate to withhold loans from foreign borrowers. Legislation for this purpose was passed in September 1965 (Public Law 89–175).
- Enlistment of the leaders of American business in a national campaign to hold down their direct investments abroad financed out of U.S. funds, their deposits in foreign banks, and their holdings of foreign financial assets. To effectuate this, the Secretary of Commerce asked some 600 of the largest businesses in the United States to set up individual balance of payments ledgers covering selected transactions, and to undertake individual programs that would bring about a 15 to 20 percent improvement in 1965 over 1964. The companies were called on to send quarterly reports on their progress to the Department of Commerce.
- Legislation to remove tax deterrents to foreign investment in U.S. securities. Legislation was passed to accomplish this (Public Law 89–809).

While some progress was made in implementing these recommendations, it or they proved inadequate or too slow. Moreover, the voluntary segment of the program had a terminal date of 1965. Accordingly, in December 1965, a revamped program was announced. Nonbank institutions, mainly business corporations, were again asked to help out in the balance of payments problems by certain actions pertaining to their foreign investments, notably repatriation of income from abroad, repatriation of short-term foreign financial assets, and the maximum use of funds obtained abroad for investment purposes. Between 500 and 600 companies had cooperated in the program in 1965. It was planned to expand this by 400 or more in 1966, so as to include more firms with direct investments of $2 million or more as of the end of 1964. A new formula was devised as a guide to individual companies in the fixing of their own direct investment targets.

Another new feature was a broadened definition of direct investments, for the purpose of application of the restraints, to have it include not only the net outflow of funds from the United States during the reporting period but also the undistributed profits of foreign subsidiaries. And finally, the list of countries classified as developed for the basic purpose was expanded.

But even these steps were not enough. The situation had not improved by the end of 1967, so in January 1968 the President issued an executive order that made mandatory some theretofore voluntary restraints. It was accompanied by proposals, requiring congressional action, and by requests on the public intended to bring into earlier effect reductions in expenditures abroad.

The executive order, dealing with certain capital transfers abroad, prohibited any person subject to jurisdiction of the United States who owns or acquires, alone or with affiliated persons, as much as 10 percent of a foreign business from engaging in any transaction involving a transfer of capital to or within any foreign country or to any foreign national outside the United States. The order also authorized the Secretary of Commerce to require such person to repatriate such part as may be specified of: (1) earnings of the foreign business attributable to such person's investment therein; and (2) bank deposits and other short-term financial assets which are held in foreign countries by or for him.

In the President's balance of payments message, released on the same date, the following operating guides were presented:

- As in the voluntary program, overall and individual company targets were to be set. Authorizations to exceed these targets were to be issued only in exceptional circumstances.
- New direct investment outflows to countries in continental Western Europe and other developed nations not heavily dependent on outside capital were to be stopped in 1968.
- New net investments in other developed countries were to be limited to 65 percent of the 1965–66 average.
- New net investments in the developing countries were to be limited to 110 percent of the 1965–66 average.

The executive order also authorized the Board of Governors of the Federal Reserve System to regulate or prohibit banks or other financial institutions from transferring capital to or within any foreign country or to any national thereof.outside the United States, and to require the repatriation by banks or financial institutions of such part as may be specified of the bank deposits or other short-term financial assets held by or for them in foreign countries. A number of authorizations and investment rules were prescribed by the Secretary of Commerce in the early months of 1968, and revised guidelines for banks and nonbank financial institutions were issued by the Federal Reserve Board, published in the *Federal Reserve Bulletin* of January 1968 and March 1968, and followed by *General Bulletin No. 1: Foreign Direct Investment Regulations,* with interpretive analysis and statements pertaining thereto, which was published in the *Federal Register* of October 10, 1968.

Chapter IV

Basic Tariff Laws and Regulations

The two basic customs laws of the United States are the Tariff Act of 1930 and the Tariff Classification Act of 1962. They specify in detail the restrictions generally imposed by the United States against each item of imported merchandise. In addition to these two basic laws, there are other important pieces of legislation whose applicability is conditional, these pertaining to Buy-American requirements, antidumping provisions, certain national security provisions, and Section 22 of the Agricultural Adjustment Act. But since they are exceptional in application and, in any case, do not rely solely on the tariff as a means of protection, they must be considered as nontariff trade barriers.

The tariff is a troublesome political issue because of its overriding domestic and important foreign policy impact. It is involved in the area in which the conflict between local and national interest is most apparent. Historically, the problem has been with us throughout the life of our country. The first act of our first Congress was the Tariff Act of 1789. Revenue was a pressing need, and there was some pressure for a protective tariff. Also, the interesting argument was made that imposition of such duties could be used to force concessions from other countries—notably England and France.

Since that time there have been many new tariffs, each of which repealed and superseded its predecessor. In its 1934 study, *The Tariff and Its History,* the Tariff Commission lists 23 principal tariff acts following the initial one of 1789. The most recent is the present law, the Tariff Act of 1930.

THE TARIFF ACT OF 1930, AS AMENDED

The Tariff Act of 1930, as amended, consists of two main divisions: Tariff Schedules of the United States, and Special and Administrative Provisions. Tariff Schedules of the United States is the legal schedule of customs duties imposed against imported merchandise. It contains some 5,250 different designations of items, some of which have been further divided for statistical purposes into a total of some 10,000 seven-digit statistical numbers. This latter system comprises the Tariff Schedules of the United States, Annotated (TSUSA), which was prepared pursuant to the Tariff Classification Act of 1962.

For each item, the following information is given in the TSUSA:

- Item number (assigned seven-digit statistical number).
- Commodity description.
- Duty status. Duty status is given in one of two columns, one being the original statutory rates established by the Tariff Act of 1930 and applying to imports from countries not entitled to reduced rates (most of the Communist-controlled countries) and the other being prevailing rates applicable to all other countries on an equal basis (except for temporary or special arrangements applicable to Cuba, the Philippines, and Canada). The second column reflects changes from the original statutory rate prescribed in the Tariff Act of 1930, based on Presidential proclamations following trade negotiations or because of specific acts of Congress, and on determinations under the Customs Simplification Act of 1954, the results of which are formalized by the Tariff Classification Act of 1962.

Following the detailed scheduling by commodity, an Appendix to the tariff schedules incorporates temporary legislation (provisions for temporary addition or amendment to the tariff schedules); temporary modifications in the schedules proclaimed pursuant to trade agreement legislation—for example, duty changes and quantitative restrictions arising from escape-clause actions; and additional import restrictions pursuant to Section 22 of the Agricultural Adjustment Act, as amended (this specifies the quantitative limitations applied under the legislation).

In order to facilitate use of the schedules and proper reporting of transactions, an alphabetical index of commodities is provided, as well as statistical annexes assigning code numbers to foreign countries and to customs districts and ports.

Special provisions. As important as the actual rates of duty, and in some cases more of a problem to the foreign trader, are the special and administrative provisions for the conduct of customs operations. These are covered in about 200 separate sections of the Tariff Act of 1930, the following being selected as typical and indicative of the general nature of their provisions:

Section	*Subject*
303	Countervailing Duties.
304	Marking of Imported Articles and Containers.
313	Drawback and Refunds.
330	Organization of the (U.S. Tariff) Commission.
336	Equalization of Costs of Production.
337	Unfair Practices in Import Trade.
338	Discrimination by Foreign Countries.
350	Promotion of Foreign Trade.

Most of the foregoing special provisions are self-explanatory by title. However, a few specific comments are appropriate.

Section 303. In some instances, exportation of certain products has been stimulated through a subsidy or other direct or indirect aid offered by the government of the producing country. This permits the individual sellers to quote lower commercial prices, with their governments making up what might otherwise be a loss on the transaction.

Subsidies are condemned by international agreement, as reflected in the General Agreement on Tariffs and Trade (GATT), which recognizes their harmful effects on import and export interests of other member countries. Accordingly, the agreement (Article XVI, Section B) calls for the contracting parties' avoiding the use of subsidies on the export of primary products and their ceasing to grant any form of subsidy on the export of any product other than a primary product when the subsidy results in the sale of such product for export at a price lower than the comparable price charged to buyers in the domestic market. In the United States, protection against this type of competition is provided by Section 303 of the Tariff Act of 1930, which provides for a countervailing duty equal to the bounty or grant received by the foreign manufacturer or exporter.

Section 336. The imposition of additional duties under prescribed conditions, of up to 50 percent of rates which have been expressly fixed by statute, is provided for in this section. But this authority has seldom been used because most of the rates in effect are fixed through negotiation, as authorized under the Trade Agreement Act of 1934.

Section 337. Under this section, goods found to be brought to the American market under unfair methods of competition, the effect or tendency of which is to destroy or substantially injure an efficient industry in the United States, are to be excluded from entry.

Section 338. New or additional duties may be prescribed by the President, if he finds that the public interest will be served thereby, upon articles produced in, or imported in a vessel of, any foreign country that imposes against U.S. products any unreasonable charge or regulation not equally enforced upon like articles of every foreign country. Similar duties may be imposed if he finds that a foreign country discriminates in fact against the commerce of the United States. This authority has never been used, which suggests that the advantage to be gained from action contemplated under it may not be as great as would be available by working out a more diplomatic resolution of the complaint.

Section 350. This is the original authority for the trade agreements program. It has been substantially amended or repealed by subsequent legislation, most recently the Trade Expansion Act of 1962.

Administrative provisions. It is under administrative provisions that procedures are prescribed, and these may give rise to the "red tape" so disliked by many. Yet the sections indicated are key ones in that they specify the rules of the road, so to speak. Some of the provisions bear detailed study by one engaged in import trade, especially the following:

Section	*Subject*
402	Valuation.
484	Entry of Merchandise.
502	Regulations for Appraisement and Classification.
505	Payment of Duties.
511	Inspection of Importers' Books.
514	Protest against Collectors' Decisions.
516	Appeal or Protest by American Producers.
526	Merchandise Bearing American Trademark.
641	Customhouse Brokers.

The few brief references that follow will serve to suggest their substance.

Section 402. Valuation of merchandise for customs purposes is perhaps the most important feature of customs laws, after the rate of duty, itself. Under U.S. law, the basis of valuation for customs purposes is as follows (except as otherwise specifically provided for) :[1]

[1] A "final list" of some 200 products continues to be valued under the original procedure specified in the Tariff Act of 1930. The main difference between that (now Section 4020) and the present procedure is that under it, goods are valued at foreign value or export value, *whichever is higher*.

- The export value.
- If the export value cannot be determined satisfactorily, then the U.S. value.
- If neither the export value nor the U.S. value can be determined satisfactorily, then the constructed value; except that in the case of an imported article subject to a rate of duty based on the American selling price, such value shall be the American selling price of such domestic article.

The section contains detailed definitions of each of these values.

The American method of valuation for customs purposes is not that used by most other countries. Practically all countries except the United States consider dutiable value to be the landed value (cost, insurance, and freight, or CIF) at the port of entry; in other words, it is valued in the import market, rather than at export, as is U.S. practice. Frequently, campaigns are undertaken to bring about a revision in the U.S. method of valuation, which, if converted to the usual foreign practice, would result in higher duties; it thus has support from those who desire more protection from foreign competition. Some also argue that the U.S. method is misleading the public insofar as our balance of trade and our trade policy are concerned. In other words, the export surplus that the United States enjoys would be less of a surplus (and might even be a deficit in some years) if statistics were reported on the same basis by the United States as by others. Of course, if the United States were to change to this method of valuation, it would call for a corresponding reduction in the specified rates of duty in order to meet demands by other countries, which would argue that without this complete modification, they would be put to disadvantage and would have to protect themselves.

Section 484. This section specifies the requirement for making an entry at the customhouse within a given time of arrival of the goods and prescribes the supporting documents needed to effect entry and release of the merchandise.

Sections 514–516. In these sections, the mechanism and procedure are outlined for protests and appeals against collectors' and customs courts' decisions; protests and appeals may be initiated either by importers or by American producers.

Section 526. This section makes it illegal to import into the United States merchandise of foreign manufacture if the merchandise bears a registered trademark owned by an American citizen or corporation, unless written consent of the owner is produced at the time of making entry. The Bureau of Customs has issued a brochure listing those products for which blanket authority to import a certain amount (especially for the benefit of tourists.) is given by the owner of the trademark.[2]

Section 641. Customhouse brokers must be licensed by the Treasury, and this section deals with such licensing. It also provides for the issuance of rules and regulations by the Secretary of the Treasury to protect importers and the revenue of the United States insofar as operations of licensed customhouse brokers are concerned.

CUSTOMS REGULATIONS OF THE UNITED STATES

To facilitate carrying out his responsibilities on a workable and uniform basis, which must be done through 46 customs collection districts with surveillance over almost 300 ports of entry, the Commissioner of Customs has issued a series of Federal Regulations (Title 19, Chapter 1). They involve a number of descriptive and procedural features and incorporate reference to appropriate Treasury decisions pertaining to the exercise of Customs' authority and responsibility. The regulations are in 56 parts, each of which includes several sections. They constitute a body of procedure and regulation that is vital to the business of importing and customs brokerage and is of direct interest to transportation companies and the foreign departments of banks.

TARIFF CLASSIFICATION ACT OF 1962

While its results are meshed into the Tariff Act of 1930 in the form of the Tariff Schedule of the United States (TSUS), some reference to this legislation is in order. There was no comprehensive revision following the Tariff Act of 1930 until the Customs Simplification Act of 1954, which directed the Tariff Commission to revise and consolidate the tariff laws in order to accomplish certain simplification objectives. The job was complex, and the guidelines within which the Tariff Commission had to work required long and tedious analysis and testimony. This is because what Congress wished was simplification of existing schedules without significant changes in tariff levels and with due consideration of our international obligations.

In developing an orderly and systematic outline, other existing systems were studied. That which evolved was a compromise, strongly influenced by the Brussels Tariff Nomenclature and the Standard Industrial Classifica-

[2] *Tourists Trademark Information,* Bureau of Customs, Washington, D.C., 1965.

tion. The former was designed primarily for duty purposes, while the latter was developed mainly for industrial and production purposes rather than for trade and distribution (see Appendix A).

Provisions of general application (previously scattered throughout the statutes) were consolidated into a set of general headnotes and rules of interpretation. There is no longer a separate free list. The Tariff Act of 1930 had several "basket" or "catchall" provisions, occasionally because articles were not specifically provided for otherwise. These were rearranged in the simplification process and out of the 15 "baskets" have come over 1,300 newly designated items. In effect, what was accomplished was: (1) a merger of all provisions of the Tariff Act of 1930 and all related provisions found in the Internal Revenue Code and elsewhere, and (2) a general internal reorganization and consolidation of basic tariff provisions so as to bring together in logical, orderly sequence all provisions affecting closely related products.

NONTARIFF TRADE BARRIERS

Many importers, here and abroad, feel they can live with customs duties, which are taxes whose postwar burden has been moderated through negotiated reductions in rates and through higher prices of goods subject to specific duty; higher prices lessen the impact of specific duties. But they do complain about barriers to trade that have nothing to do with comparative price. For these say, in effect, "Regardless of how efficient you are or for what price you can sell, the market is closed to you for other reasons." Sometimes the market is open for a certain amount or quantity (in some cases negotiated between governments, or based on historical record); at other times, the availability of the market is adjusted to changed conditions, but with reference to factors other than price—such as foreign exchange availability or domestic production of the product in question.

What this all means is that an exporter cannot justify the expenditure of time and money to cultivate a market aggressively if the market is subject to being closed off for reasons other than price. And an importer cannot, himself, justify the time and expense to advertise and otherwise build up demand for an imported product if he is liable to find his sources of supply at the best price shut off.

The types of nontariff trade barriers are numerous and varied, as are the reasons, actual or ostensible, for their employment. Merely identifying them positively is difficult, since some are only potential barriers, whose restrictive effect arises from procedures, regulations, and administration. The following is a list of practices or institutions in the administration of which opportunity exists for discrimination among supplier countries:

- Government procurement practices.
- Quantitative restrictions (and import licensing).
- Arbitrary valuation practices for imposition of duties.
- State trading.
- Subsidies to domestic producers.
- Health, safety, and sanitary regulations.
- Marking and labeling requirements.
- Advance deposits required of importers.
- Reservation of part of market to satisfy bilateral trade agreements.
- Advertising restrictions—as on alcoholic beverages.
- Milling and mixing requirements.
- Variable import levies.
- Licensing of foreign exchange transactions.
- Multiple exchange rates.
- Antidumping legislation and regulation.
- Embargoes.

Some of the foregoing are far-reaching in importance and others are of no more than nuisance value. The most pernicious to private world trade, based on relative costs, are quantitative restrictions—quotas and their companion import-licensing regimes—and exchange controls. Both of these latter are usually rationalized as necessary because of the employing country's foreign exchange position. In any case, the use of some is spasmodic, in point of time, coming into and going out of employment with changes in commercial policy and other conditions, and some are employed by only one country. Others are more widely used.

A survey published by the Department of Commerce in 1966[3] showed that licensing of imports is widely practiced in the less-developed countries, and that many, if not most, also practice exchange controls. Licensing is required for the importation of relatively few products into the developed countries. In addition to the licensing and control of exchange transactions, some countries require a prior deposit of cash (up to a stated percentage of the value of the goods to be imported) at the time the import license is applied for; this amounts to the importer's having to pay in advance—some-

[3] "Worldwide Import Rules Summarized for Traders," *International Commerce Magazine,* U.S. Department of Commerce, Washington, D.C., August 29, 1966, pp. 2–8.

times far in advance—for receipt of the goods to be imported. This can only, and is intended to, serve to discourage imports.

Removal or reduction of such trade barriers is not easy as a matter of negotiation because it is so difficult to equate the monetary values of concessions given or received. Nevertheless, in the Trade Expansion Act of 1962, the President was given authority to proclaim the modification or continuance of ". . . any existing duty or *other import restriction*" (the italics added). Liberal use of this provision became questionable, however, as in 1966 the Senate passed a resolution asking that no antidumping agreement be negotiated without authorization of Congress—that is, that it not be entered as part of an executive agreement under the Trade Expansion Act.

U.S. EMPLOYMENT OF NONTARIFF TRADE BARRIERS

A mere scanning of the list in the preceding section will suggest that the United States is not a major employer of nontariff trade barriers. Only a few of the major restrictions listed are used to any extent by the United States.

Among the major U.S. nontariff trade barriers (or what may at times be regarded as such by foreign exporters) one finds the following:

- Buy-American legislation.
- Antidumping legislation.
- National security provisions in trade policy.
- Pure food and drug laws.
- Marking and labeling requirements.
- Quotas or embargoes imposed for agricultural price support purposes, for conservation, or for safety.

The comments pertaining to each deal with its origin, its manner of being implemented, and with recent experience in its employment.

Buy-American legislation. Some Federal legislation, and procurement legislation in several states, requires that preference in public procurement be given domestic materials. This Federal policy originated in the early 1930's; it is not made effective by a separate law but by a provision of continuing effect enacted initially as an amendment to the Treasury and Post Office Appropriations Act for 1934.[4] The act was signed on March 3, 1933, and is commonly referred to as the Buy-American Act of 1933.

[4] This review is based substantially on a paper prepared in 1960 by the Office of the General Counsel of the Department of Commerce for the use of the Commerce Field Offices.

Briefly stated, the law requires U.S. Government agencies to procure only domestic materials unless: (1) they are for use outside the United States or its territories; (2) they are not available in sufficient quantities and of sufficient quality; (3) the head of the agency determines their purchase would be "inconsistent with the public interest"; or (4) he determines their cost to be unreasonable.

Prior to 1954 there was no uniformity between all the procurement agencies, but they generally followed a policy of considering unreasonable a domestic bid when it exceeded the price of the foreign article, duty paid, by more than 25 percent. In December 1954, Executive Order 10582 was issued to prescribe uniform procedures for all determinations under the Buy-American legislation. This order specifies that the offer of a domestic supplier is to be considered unreasonable if it exceeds the foreign offered price by more than 6 percent, duty paid and delivered. It also provides the alternative computation of 10 percent differential over foreign materials *exclusive* of duty.

The order further provides for exceptions to the 6 percent (and 10 percent) rule in cases involving: (1) special reasons of national interest; (2) procurement from small business; (3) procurement in areas of substantial unemployment; and (4) protection of essential national security interests. Since November 1955, the policy has been established that the maximum *additional* differential for purchases in areas of substantial unemployment, as designated by the Secretary of Labor, shall be 6 percent, so that the total differential would be 12 percent. Under exception (1), above, agency heads can apply higher differentials when they determine that it is not unreasonable or inconsistent with the public interest.

In 1962, when attention became centered on the balance of payments problem, the Defense Department, our biggest purchaser of foreign goods, decided to abandon the 6–12 formula, whether the procurement was for domestic or foreign usage, and adopted instead a 50 percent differential as a benchmark. This, of course, caused other countries to complain that this important segment of our market is cut off from them—and it is. Many other countries, on the other hand, themselves follow preferential treatment for their own economies, but do so through administrative decisions rather than through specific and open law.

Other pieces of legislation that specifically require preferential treatment for domestic suppliers include:

- A proviso in the annual Defense Appropriations Act (often referred to as the Berry Amendment) that no part of the appropriation shall be available for the purchase of any article of food or clothing not grown or produced in the United States or its possessions, except to the extent that the Secretary of the Department concerned shall determine that a satisfactory quality and sufficient quantity cannot be procured at U.S. market prices without unduly increasing future U.S. market prices. Certain exceptions are listed, but the discretion is narrower than under the Buy-American legislation.

- The Strategic and Critical Materials Stockpiling Act of 1946, which requires that purchases of strategic and critical materials be made in accordance with provisions of the Buy-American Act of 1933.
- The Merchant Marine Act of 1936, which provides that, so far as practicable, only materials of the growth, production, or manufacture of the United States shall be used in ship construction under a construction-differential subsidy.
- A provision in Federal housing legislation, which subjects the use of funds made available for carrying out the work of the United States Housing Administration to restrictions under the Buy-American Act.

Antidumping legislation. "Dumping" is the term used to identify the practice of some exporters of selling abroad at less than the comparable price in the home market; the offsetting special rate which may be invoked is called the antidumping duty.

The act comes into operation when: (1) a foreign producer sells to U.S. importers at a price less than that which he charges in certain other markets, and (2) there is resultant injury to U.S. industry. Price discrimination typically involves a lower price in the United States than is charged in the foreign producer's *home* market. However, if the producer is principally an exporter, price discrimination is found if there is a lower price to the United States than to third countries—that is, the price charged in the producer's export sales other than to the United States. If, on the other hand, the foreign producer sells only to the United States, price discrimination will be found if the U.S. price is lower than the producer's cost. Price discrimination is to be determined by the Secretary of the Treasury.

Injury will be found if an industry in the United States is hurt or is likely to be hurt, or is prevented from being established, by imports which involve price discrimination. The existence or likelihood of such an injury is determined by the Tariff Commission. In 12 years, 1955–1966, 356 claims were filed with the U.S. Treasury. The finding of dumping was positive in only 11 cases.[5] In 224 of the cases, no price discrimination was found; in 81 cases, price revision or termination of sales ended the complaint; and in 40 cases, no injury was found. Hence there have been accusations that the American antidumping mechanism is not adequately effective. This area of discontent manifested itself by the introduction of a series of rather identical bills in the 89th Congress (1965–66) to amend the Antidumping Act by establishing more narrowly defined injury criteria and establishing detailed statutory procedures for the conduct of investigations pertaining to them.

Antidumping duties are lifted when the complaint on which they were based has been corrected or removed, but as of mid-1967, they were in effect on the following items:[6]

- Australia—chromic acid.
- Belgium, Portugal, Sweden, and the Dominican Republic—portland cement, other than white, nonstaining.
- Canada—steel reinforcing bars, carbon steel bars and structural shapes, and steel jacks.
- Japan—asobisformamide.

The practice of dumping is condemned by international agreement through Article VI, Section 1, of the GATT, which defines the practice as introducing the products of one country into the commerce of another country at less than the normal value of the products. By definition of the condemned practices, due allowance is to be made for differences in conditions and terms of sale, for differences in taxation, and for other differences affecting price comparability.

One of the accomplishments of the Kennedy Round was the negotiation of an internationally agreed antidumping code, which supplements the provisions of GATT Article VI with rules and procedures to be followed in antidumping actions. But Public Law 90–634 still preserves the U.S. Tariff Commission's antidumping prerogatives. The principal advantages of the antidumping code to the United States were reported by the Office of the Special Representative for Trade Negotiations to be: (1) the adoption by other countries of fair and open procedures along the lines of U.S. practices, and (2) the adoption by Canada of an injury requirement in its antidumping legislation. The lack of such a requirement had impeded U.S. exports for many years.

National security provisions. The interrelationship of national security and trade policy appears to have initially been recognized formally in the

[5] James Pomeroy Hendrick, Deputy Assistant Secretary of the Treasury, *Administration of the United States Antidumping Act,* mimeographed memorandum released by U.S. Treasury Department, 1966.

[6] Source: Bureau of Customs, U.S. Treasury Department.

Trade Agreements Extension Act of 1954. It was spelled out more fully and precisely in 1955. It is now included as Section 232 of the Trade Expansion Act of 1962, which reads, "No action shall be taken . . . to decrease or eliminate the duty or other import restriction on any article if the President determines that such reduction or elimination would threaten to impair the national security."

This particular feature provides that upon request of the head of any government agency or department, upon application of any interested party, or on his own motion, the Director of the Office of Emergency Planning shall make an investigation to determine the effects on the national security of import of the article which is the subject of such request, application, or motion. If unfavorable, he shall advise the President, and the President, unless he determines that the article is *not* being imported in such quantities and in such circumstances as to threaten or impair the national security, shall take such action as he deems necessary to adjust such imports so that they will not threaten to impair the national security.

As of 1967, about 35 requests for investigation had been filed, and there had been only one affirmative finding—on petroleum, oil products, and derivatives (crude oil, unfinished oil, petroleum products). An investigation was under way in 1966 and 1967 to see whether the restriction should be retained or lifted.

Pure food and drug laws. Many complaints have been registered by importers because of application of the food and drug laws. At times the complaint is heard that these laws are such a restriction on imports that trading cannot be carried on, or that foreign exporters find the laws obnoxious and that compliance with them is not worth the cost. It is advisable that the facts of such a general complaint be understood, and also that appreciation be had that the food and drug laws are not aimed at foreign goods alone.

The Federal Food, Drug, and Cosmetics Act of 1938 is the basic law under which this restriction operates. It provides for supervision of traffic in food, drugs, and cosmetics in order to safeguard public health. No distinction is made between domestic and foreign goods in its application. Yet it is listed as a nontariff trade barrier merely because it has been so interpreted by many foreigners. However, when the point is made to them that the law and regulations do not apply only to imports, their criticism moderates.

Marking and labeling requirements. Many foreign traders feel that what might appear to be minor regulatory measures or precautions are even greater obstacles to the international movement of goods than is the tariff rate. One of these pertains to marks of origin. Marks-of-origin regulations in the United States devolve from the Tariff Act of 1930, and many foreign countries have employed varying types of similar regulation, examples of which are the stamping, painting, or indelible impression as to country of origin on each piece of pottery; die stamping or embossing of each thermometer; the indelible marking of cotton towels; the marking as to country of origin of each separate pencil, chalk, or crayon; and the marking of individual imported eggs as to country of origin.

The justification for requiring marks of origin on goods offered for public sale can serve no *economic* purpose; if such a purpose were to be served, distinguishing marks would be attached somewhere along the production or distribution line without compulsion. But manufacturers often are unable to know, at the time of production, to which foreign country, if any at all, the goods will be sold. The marking then becomes a supplemental expense after the goods come off the production line, increasing their cost.

Other import legislation. It will have been seen that much of the legislation pertaining to imports has been directed toward regulating foreign goods' access to the U.S. market via the tariff and occasionally through the use of other constraints, fiscal or otherwise. There are also some special safeguards issued against harmful trade practices or based on sensitive domestic, political, and economic considerations. Such special arrangements are primarily of the nonfiscal trade barrier type. Their variety and number are typified by the following restrictions in force as of 1965:

- Absolute quotas and embargoes may be imposed pursuant to Section 22 of the Agricultural Adjustment Act, as amended, if importation renders or tends to render ineffective or materially interferes with programs of the U.S. Department of Agriculture relating to agricultural commodities.
- The Sugar Act of 1948, as amended, authorizes the Secretary of Agriculture to determine the annual domestic sugar requirements and to assign prorated market quotas to domestic areas and foreign countries on the basis of a formula included in the legislation.
- The Philippine Trade Agreement of 1946, as revised, provides for absolute quotas on imports of certain products imported from the Philippines, which products enjoy a preferential rate of duty that is being phased out.
- Quotas and embargoes are provided for other products for reasons such as conservation (eggs and feathers of most wild birds) or safety (white phosphorous matches).
- Quantitative limitations on imports are also required by or may be imposed under intergovernmental commodity agreements to which the United States is party. Among these are cotton textiles, cotton textile products, and coffee.

Chapter V

Commercial Treaties and Trade Agreements

Many governments seek, by treaty or agreement, enlarged trading opportunities that are nondiscriminatory as between supplier countries and that are rather clearly spelled out in advance. Businessmen can then plan their commitments with more certainty as to what to expect.

Both treaties and agreements seek the same goal, but there is a significant difference between them based on legal considerations. The first type, commercial *treaties,* are formal treaties which, by due process of being ratified by the Senate (as far as the United States is concerned), become the law of the land. The second, trade *agreements,* are no less binding on business conduct, but their legality is sometimes questioned. Adherence to the agreements, made by the executive branch of the Government, is conditional on their being consistent with appropriate law. They are properly called "executive agreements," entered into by the President under authority given him by Congress.

A fundamental point in international business is that engaging in business transactions in a country other than one's own is a privilege and not a right. Usually, this privilege and the delineation of its conditions are worked out by negotiation between governments. This is not to say that without prior negotiation between governments, private business interests may not enter into or conduct business abroad. They may, but the conditions under which they can do so are not defined by treaty between governments; therefore, the conditions do not take on the character of legal rights in the enforcement of which one may have to call on his own government for assistance.

This privilege of doing business in a foreign country and the conditions under which it is formally granted are the substance of a series of treaties known in the United States as Treaties of Friendship, Commerce, and Navigation. In some cases they are titled otherwise, such as Treaty of Establishment, or Convention to Regulate Commerce and Navigation. In any case they are by nature commercial treaties.

Guaranties of security of rights in property, of course, are of special importance to the American who goes abroad as a businessman. Without such guaranties the economic privileges given to him by a treaty would lose much of their meaning. With them, however, the treaty comes to be a code of fair treatment for the American businessman who seeks to trade, to invest, or to run a business in a foreign country.

The objective of commercial treaties is to gain and secure opportunities in foreign markets for another nation's products and investments on a nondiscriminatory basis, as a general rule. But the main consideration is not privilege as compared with nationals of the host country; it is privilege no less favorable than that granted other foreigners. Such privileges are exchanged in the negotiation, with the governments granting and guaranteeing reciprocal privileges to each other's nationals.

In order to facilitate this objective, provision is made for granting opportunity of entry and specific personal protection to the citizens of each country in the territory of the other. The provisions for acquisition of property and security of the rights therein are of special importance to foreign investors and to the personnel needed in the establishment and conduct of such enterprises.

Commercial treaties between states encompass an extensive variety of subjects having to do with the treatment to be accorded to persons, to means of communication and transportation, and to commerce in general. Specific provisions are found in these treaties for such matters as immigration and emigration; conditions of residence, travel, employment, and trade; imposition of taxes; navigation, harbor, and quarantine regulations; industrial property rights (patents, trademarks, and copyrights); and tariffs and customs laws pertaining to import and export trade.

Desirability of equality of treatment, or nondiscrimination. Equality of treatment is justified and demanded on grounds of economic theory and of harmonious international relations. It affords more opportunity to specialize in the production of that which one can turn out relatively most efficiently and to benefit from the economies of scale; and when all countries are treated alike in commercial matters, the possibility of international tension and conflict is reduced. The history of nondiscriminatory treatment in commercial relations, in the most-favored-nation context, is largely that of the granting of equal tariff treatment, since the tariff has been historically the device most frequently used by the major trading nations to protect certain domestic producers from import competition. However, the evolution of several more direct trade restrictions in the postwar period and negotiated reductions in the rates of duty appear certain to reduce materially the role of tariffs in future commercial policy questions.

The most-favored-nation principle. Since the objective of modern commercial treaties is to open doors for international business opportunities on a nondiscriminatory basis (except where customs unions and free trade areas are being established), and since such treaties commonly apply to a wide range of, if not all, products entering a nation's foreign trade, it would appear that the most-favored-nation (MFN) clause contained in them should apply to all types of trade barriers. This is the case; a number of commercial treaties and agreements provide for MFN treatment beyond simple tariff rates. Typical of this broader coverage is Article XIV of the Treaty of Friendship, Commerce, and Navigation (1956) between the United States and the Netherlands, which reads as follows:

> Each party shall accord most-favored-nation treatment to products of the other party, from whatever place and by whatever type of carrier arriving, and to products destined for exportation to the territories of such other party, by whatever route and by whatever type of carrier, with respect to customs duties and charges of any kind imposed on or in connection with importation or exportation or imposed on the international transfer of payments for imports or exports, and with respect to the method of levying such duties and charges, and with respect to all rules and formalities in connection with importation and exportation.
>
> Neither party shall impose restrictions or prohibitions on the importation of any product of the other party, or on the exportation of any product to the territories of the other party, unless the importation of the like product of, or the exportation of the like product to, all third countries is similarly restricted or prohibited.

On a broader front, the General Agreement on Tariffs and Trade calls, with certain specified exceptions, for a policy of nondiscrimination in all areas.

The administration of nontariff trade barriers need not be discriminatory. Policy may be absolutely nondiscriminatory. However, effective nondiscrimination depends on the goodwill of all levels of authority in a country imposing quantitative limitations, as the opportunity is great for administrative diversions which can rarely be effectively challenged by another country whose exporters may feel that they were not given fair treatment in, for example, the issuance of licenses. In any case, one of the certain results of such a restriction is discouragement to aggressive market development because the door may be barred without much notice, and with immediate or potentially paralyzing results.

Conditional and unconditional MFN. The principle of nondiscrimination in international business opportunities is important not only in the gaining of such opportunities, but in the securing of them after they have been gained. The most effective method of doing this is by incorporation of the principle through what is commonly called the most-favored-nation clause. This is included in all Treaties of Friendship, Commerce, and Navigation to which the United States is a partner; in reciprocal trade agreements made by the United States; and it is a cornerstone of the General Agreement on Tariffs and Trade. The MFN clause not only provides that nondiscrimination is agreed, but it specifies how its continuance is to be achieved, in case either partner to the treaty or agreement subsequently extends favorable treatment to a third country. Continuance of MFN treatment may be on a *conditional* or on an *unconditional* basis.

A variant to the strict application of nondiscrimination is that legally a country may be required to extend MFN treatment only to other countries that undertake the same obligation, such as do the contracting parties to the GATT. But nothing except its own policy is to prevent a country from extending MFN treatment to all others—from following a policy of strict nondiscrimination except when another discriminates against it. This the United States does. We extend nondiscriminatory or most-favored-nation, treatment to all countries, whether GATT members or not, provided only that they do not discriminate against us. Thus products of Mexico, not a GATT contracting party and a country with which we have no bilateral commercial arrangement into which the MFN principle could be incorporated, are subject to the same duty in the United States as are those of GATT countries. But Mexico does not discriminate against U.S. exports, as do certain Communist countries. These latter, then, and they alone, do not receive MFN treatment from the United States. Temporary preferential arrangements in favor of the Philippines are extended by the United States, which also is party to a special preferential arrangement with Canada on automotive parts.

Methods of achieving equality of treatment. The United States receives and grants MFN treatment with respect to customs duties by both multilateral and bilateral contract. As shown in Exhibit 20, it is party to agreements or treaties with over 100 countries that specify MFN treatment for American products in their markets and for their products in U.S. customs

EXHIBIT 20

TREATIES AND AGREEMENTS PROVIDING MFN TREATMENT FOR U.S. EXPORTS, 1967

MFN treatment provided for through being a Contracting Party, fully or provisionally, to the GATT (also provided for by bilateral treaty or agreement).*

Argentina	Ghana	Nigeria
Australia	*Greece	*Norway
*Austria	Guyana	*Pakistan
Barbados	Haiti	Peru
*Belgium	*Iceland	Poland
Brazil	India	*Portugal
Burma	Indonesia	Rhodesia
Burundi	Israel	Rwanda
*Cambodia	*Italy	Senegal
Cameroon	Ivory Coast	Sierra Leone
Canada	Jamaica	South Africa
Central African Republic	*Japan	*Spain
Ceylon	Kenya	Sweden
Chad	Korea	*Switzerland & Lichtenstein
Chile	Kuwait	Tanzania
Congo	Luxembourg	Togo
*Cuba	Madagascar	Trinidad and Tobago
Cyprus	Malawi	*Tunisia
Czechoslovakia	Malaysia	*Turkey
Dahomey	Malta	Uganda
*Denmark	Mauritania	*United Arab Republic
Dominican Republic	*Netherlands	*United Kingdom
*Finland	New Zealand	Upper Volta
*France	*Nicaragua	Uruguay
Gabon	Niger	*Yugoslavia
Gambia		
Germany, Federal Republic of		

MFN treatment achieved via bilaterial treaty or agreement, and not encompassed in the GATT (non-Contracting Parties to GATT).

Albania	Iran	Nepal
Bolivia	Iraq	Paraguay
Brunei	Ireland	Philippines
China, Republic of	Latvia	Saudi Arabia
Colombia	Lebanon	Syria
Costa Rica	Liberia	Thailand
El Salvador	Lithuania	Venezuela
Estonia	Morocco	Viet Nam
Ethiopia	Muscat	Yemen
Honduras		

MFN treatment dependent on affiliation with GATT on basis other than as a Contracting Party (countries which maintain a de facto application of the GATT pending final decisions as to their future commercial policy).

Algeria	Lesotho	Poland
Botswana	Maldive Islands	Singapore
Congo, Democratic Republic of	Mali	Zambia

Source: U.S. Department of State.

territory. Of this number, 76 or more countries obtain from us and give to us the assurance of MFN treatment through the instrument of the GATT; and several of these countries also effect this provision by means of bilateral trade agreements apart from the GATT obligation. The first bilateral treaty was the U.S.-French commercial agreement of 1778. This was followed by some 130 other bilateral treaties over the next century and a half, and at times and as conditions permitted, the State Department program of commercial treaties has been more actively pursued than at others.

The privileges or assurances sought changed with the times. In the earlier days the opportunity to trade at all and the right of American vessels to engage in foreign commerce were of compelling interest. Later motivations had political origin, such as in the case of a number of treaties negotiated with newly formed Latin American countries in the 1820's. This was not only part of our prompt recognition of these states, but was in substance an effective bolstering of the Monroe Doctrine.[1] More recently, investment and licensing (establishment privileges) have demanded as much, and perhaps more, attention. This was related not only to the great postwar expansion of U.S. private investments abroad, much of which was in developed areas. Congress, in the Mutual Security Act of 1954, specifically directed the executive branch to accelerate the program for negotiating such treaties in order to encourage and facilitate the flow of private investment to countries participating in the Mutual Security Program.[2]

The bilateral *treaties* are more encompassing than are the straight *trade agreements,* as they concern themselves with many more subjects, as mentioned earlier. Some of the existing bilateral treaties amended or modified earlier ones in order to take care of newly evolved mutual interests. As of mid-1967, bilateral treaties to which the United States is party, were in force or in process with the following countries:[3]

Concluded before 1920

Argentina
Bolivia
Brunei
Colombia
Costa Rica
Morocco
Paraguay
Spain
Switzerland
United Kingdom
Yugoslavia

[1] *Commercial Treaty Program of the United States,* Department of State Publication 6565, Commercial Policy Series 163, released January 1958, p. 3.
[2] *Ibid.,* p. 6.
[3] Source: U.S. Department of State.

Concluded 1920–1945

Austria	Latvia
Estonia	Liberia
Finland	Norway
Honduras	Turkey
Iraq	

Concluded since 1945

Belgium	Italy
China, Republic of	Japan
Denmark	Korea
Ethiopia	Luxembourg
France	Muscat and Oman
Germany, Federal Republic of	Netherlands
Greece	Nicaragua
Iran	Pakistan
Ireland	Thailand
Israel	Vietnam

TRADE AGREEMENTS

One of the obstacles frequently faced by exporters is the existence of bilateral trade agreements among countries other than their own, through the operation of which they are disadvantaged because trade in their product is channeled one way or the other by prearrangement between governments.

Bilateral trade agreements are still widely used; notably, as between certain of the Free World and Soviet Bloc countries; between less-developed countries and certain of the industrial countries; and as between less-developed countries themselves.[4] Some agreements may call for actual barter. Others may provide for guaranteed or preferential licensing of imports of specified quantities of specified products, such as may be of export interest to the partner country. In many cases quotas are set up on a geographical basis

[4] The International Monetary Fund reports, in its *Fifteenth Annual Report on Exchange Restrictions* (p. 3), that on March 31, 1964, there were 310 bilateral payments agreements involving Fund member countries actively in operation. Many of these are related to trade agreements that provide for the exchange of designated quantities of specified goods.

in order to accommodate to bilateral trade agreements entered into between the importing (licensing) country and one or more countries supplying the product.

The United States, which espouses private, nondiscriminatory trade, has not been active in bilateral trade arrangements of the type that call for the exchange of a certain amount of designated products for a certain amount of other designated products. Rather, its position has been to oppose them in principle and, in fact, not to negotiate on them. Diplomatic representations are, of course, made if U.S. commercial interests are unduly hampered by the agreements entered into by others. On the other hand, the United States has laid the groundwork for expanding its exports by following a strong program of trade agreements—commonly called reciprocal trade agreements—the object of which is not to specify particular products to be exchanged in agreed amounts, but to negotiate for the reduction of trade barriers on a broad front, thus opening a variety of trading opportunities for private business.

The reciprocal trade agreements program. The cornerstone of U.S. action in this area is a section of the Tariff Act of 1930 (Section 350, titled "Promotion of Export"). This section has as its basic objective authorization of the negotiation of export trade opportunities.

On June 12, 1934, the Tariff Act of 1930 was amended by signing of the Reciprocal Tariff Bill (better known as the Reciprocal Trade Agreements Act), under which the President was given authority to enter into foreign trade agreements with foreign governments or instrumentalities thereof. This authority was limited in time to three years and was circumscribed to a reduction or an increase not to exceed 50 percent of the duty specified in the Tariff Act of 1930.

This was a significant turning point in our tariff history, for it meant that for the first time Congress (the legislative branch) delegated to the President (the executive branch) the function of setting certain exact rates of duty over a practically unlimited range of products without requiring the prior or subsequent approval of either the Senate or the Congress. Even though the authority was within clearly prescribed limitations, one heard and still hears voices of protest against this action, along lines that Congress abrogated its constitutional responsibility, and that the whole procedure is therefore illegal and unconstitutional.

The fact is that at the time of passage of this act the international business community was faced with a veritable network of exchange controls, licensing, barter deals, trade agreements, higher duties, and the like. If an American exporter sought to sell abroad, the foreign buyer often had to find out from his government whether purchases could be made from Americans, or whether he had to buy from a supplier in some other country with which a bilateral trade agreement had been entered into or whose exchange was available through his licensing authorities. This was obviously something that could not be corrected overnight. On the commercial policy side, as contrasted with the financial, it involved trading away of policies by two or more countries—the mutual uprooting of protection against competition. It meant subordinating local domestic preference to the national interest—taking away preferred positions from some producers in order to give competitive opportunities to others.

The assumption was accepted that expansion of trade is desirable, meaning, particularly in this case, *foreign* trade. But one country could not and cannot do what is necessary alone, just in the hope that others may eventually follow suit. There obviously had to be a negotiated reduction in trade barriers, a reciprocal one, in which it could be said, "We offer you this if you will give us that in exchange." Naturally, this had to be done by someone competent to negotiate, someone with competence based on legal authority. This is the rationale for the legislative branch's authorizing the executive branch of the government to undertake these negotiations. The first such broad act, now extended 12 times, was the Trade Agreements Act of 1934.

This act marked a break in the procedure for setting tariff rates, as employed in the 150 years preceding 1934. But the most important break appears not to have been in procedure or mechanics, but in objective—in the concept of exchanging broad tariff concessions for mutual benefit. In effect, the United States deliberately legislated for trade expansion.

Under this legislation and its several extensions, the United States entered into a number of reciprocal trade agreements, at first bilaterally negotiated. During the three years for which the authority was originally granted, 16 agreements were concluded. Subsequent renewals or extensions of the authority resulted in additional negotiations, all of which were bilateral. But on the strength of authority in the 1945 renewal of the act, the United States stimulated simultaneous, bilateral negotiations with and between a number of countries. The results of these negotiations, conducted in Geneva in 1947, and the benefits of which were extended multilaterally on a most-favored-nation basis, were included in a General Agreement on Tariffs and Trade.

Effect on average duty levels. The end result of the series of negotiations since 1934 has been a steady reduction in the level of U.S. duties (see Exhibit 21).

Clearly, the United States is not a high-tariff country; and the further reductions negotiated in the Kennedy Round will mean a further lowering of average U.S. duty levels. Overly positive and overly precise conclusions must, however, be guarded against because: (1) as the proportion of duty-

EXHIBIT 21

RATIOS OF DUTIES COLLECTED TO VALUE OF IMPORTS ENTERED FOR CONSUMPTION 1926 TO 1966

	Duties collected as	
Yearly average or year	*Percent of Total Imports*	*Percent of Dutiable Imports*
1926-30	14	40
1931-35	18	50
1936-40	15	38
1941-45	11	32
1946-50	7	16
1951-55	5	12
1956-60	7	11
1961	7	12
1962	8	12
1963	7	12
1964	7	12
1965	8	12
1966	8	12

Source: *Statistical Abstract of the United States*, Table 1235, U. S. Department of Commerce, Washington, D. C., 1967.

free imports increases, the tendency must be for the ratio of duties collected against total imports to decline; (2) as prices of dutiable imported goods increase, the ratio of duties collected to imports will decrease where the duty is *specific*—that is, based on physical units, rather than *ad valorem*—that is, based on value; and (3) high duties may so discourage imports as effectively to block them out. Since the ratios are calculated by comparing the duties actually collected with the values of goods actually imported for consumption, the true impact of duty changes may be obscured.

Trade Expansion Act of 1962. The twelfth extension and amendment of the Trade Agreements Act of 1934 is known as the Trade Expansion Act of 1962. It is the authority under which the Kennedy Round of GATT negotiations was conducted in 1965–67, and the legislation by which the United States sought to have the Common Market and European Free Trade Area countries, especially, lower their barriers so the preferences they give each other would put us to less disadvantage.

There were two major parts to the bill, one dealing with negotiating authority and the other dealing with assistance to firms, workers, and industries in adjusting to conditions resulting from action taken by the President in carrying out trade agreements. One significant departure found in this act as compared with its predecessors was the right to eliminate certain duties altogether, thus placing the items on the free list. Actual negotiation, under authority of the President, was conducted under the direct supervision of the Special Representative for Trade Negotiations.

The provisions for import adjustment assistance were a new feature, designed to spread the impact of adjusting to bigger volumes so the burden would not be concentrated industrially or geographically. The arrangements would, in effect, supplant the escape clause procedure, the cost of whose protection is borne solely by consumers of the imported or protected product through higher prices. Industrywide protection is still available, through a modified escape clause procedure, but it is anticipated that such assistance will be forthcoming only when assistance to firms and workers would be inadequate to mitigate widespread injury to the industry. The Trade Expansion Act of 1962 thus represented a fundamental change in the American attitude toward injury from foreign competition. In the 1934 act and its successors, the basic view was that no one was really supposed to be hurt as a result of trade concessions that it was hoped would stimulate export opportunities. Protection against such injury would be provided by withdrawing the concession—by escape clause action. But under the 1962 version of the bill, injury was accepted and expected. Assistance was to be offered not by closing off the competition from abroad, but by aiding the firms and workers involved to retrain, relocate, and readjust—not necessarily to making the same item as before.

The General Agreement on Tariffs and Trade. The broadest and most unique trade agreement ever to come into existence is the General Agreement on Tariffs and Trade (GATT), which was negotiated in Geneva, in 1947, by the United States and 22 other countries.[5] GATT was the first multination attempt to reduce tariffs and other obstacles to trade on a reciprocal basis. It came into being in an effort to accelerate the lowering of tariffs and the reduction of other obstacles to trade, pending completion and ratification of the proposed Havana Charter for an International Trade Organization.[6]

[5] Seventy-six countries had acceded to the agreement, in full or provisionally, as of early 1968, and eleven additional countries have acceded to the GATT provisionally, participate in its work by special arrangement, or maintain a *de facto* application of it, pending final decisions as to their future commercial policies.

[6] This organization never saw the light of day. Ratification was requested by the President but was not given by Congress, so in 1950 the request for ratification was withdrawn. Congressional expressions concerning GATT usually refer to it as "the executive agreement known as the General Agreement on Tariffs and Trade." GATT has never achieved the status of being a treaty.

Under terms of the agreement, concessions granted in any of the negotiations would inure to the benefit of all countries signatory to the agreement. Thus the United States received benefits not only from the 15 negotiations in which it participated directly but also from the 91 other negotiations carried out by other countries. Under the auspices of GATT, several other multilateral trade negotiations have taken place, the most recent being the Kennedy Round, completed substantially in 1967.

A second reason for GATT's special significance is that it went beyond merely negotiating the reduction of trade barriers. It incorporated a number of "general provisions" having to do with policy and the long-range conditions of trade. This feature appears to have been the one which caused difficulty in its being ratified as a treaty. Its critics felt that by executive negotiation, the hands of Congress were being tied, and that Congress was being asked to ratify an agreement pertaining to a number of points specifying the conditions of trade as well as of taxation, and this it would not do.

Part I of the GATT incorporates the most-favored-nation clause in its unconditional and unlimited form. This was not in conflict with U.S. law. Part II was considered to be treading on thin ice. It deals with the use of barriers to trade other than tariffs. It specifies the principle of reciprocal national treatment on internal taxes and regulations, lays down rules confining the use of antidumping and countervailing duties, sets out a definition of "actual" value for customs purposes, establishes a principle to be followed in connection with exporting and importing formalities, and provides for the liberalization of marks-of-origin regulations. Considerable attention is also given the problem of quantitative restrictions and exchange controls. This part represents something in the nature of a *de facto* policy among the contracting governments regarding the use of quantitative restrictions, and it outlines a set of rules governing their employment as a means of adjusting balance of payments difficulties. In addition, the use of exchange controls is similarly restricted as a matter of policy. Other problems covered in this part have to do with subsidies and programs for economic development, the general rule being to keep other contracting parties informed.

Part III deals with procedural matters, modification of schedules, relation of the agreement to the proposed International Trade Organization, amendments, and withdrawals. Part IV, which concerns itself primarily with trade of the less-developed countries, was negotiated in 1964 and became a legal part of GATT in 1966 upon its acceptance by two-thirds of the contracting parties. Its main substantive provision is that the developed countries, recognizing the role of international trade in economic development, and recognizing the need for positive efforts to ensure that developing countries secure a share in the growth in international trade commensurate with their needs for economic development, will accord high priority to the reduction and elimination of barriers to products currently or potentially of particular export interest to less-developed contracting parties, including customs duties and other restrictions which differentiate unreasonably between such products in their primary and in their processed forms. This part also incorporates the provision that the developed contracting parties do not expect reciprocity for commitments made by them in trade negotiations to reduce or remove tariffs and other barriers to the trade of less-developed contracting parties.

Under the protocol of provisional application, the United States and a few other key countries undertook "to apply provisionally on and after January 1948, (a) Parts I and III of the Agreement, and (b) Part II of the Agreement to the fullest extent not inconsistent with existing legislation."[7] Thus, though not a treaty, the GATT is a very important element in international trade. In addition to being an executive agreement with corresponding legal force, it provides for an international forum that regularly, if not continuously, permits a confrontation between countries concerning their trading opportunities in the markets of other countries. Its statement of principles, though not all have been incorporated legally, constitutes the only widely agreed code of conduct in international business relations.

INTERNATIONAL COMMODITY ARRANGEMENTS

International commodity arrangements may be defined as agreements or undertakings between governments, having to do with production, exporting, importing, pricing, or other marketing practices relating to a commodity. National and international regulatory schemes have generally developed from the accumulation of large stocks, which could not be disposed of at economic levels because of declines in price. The social consequences of price fluctuations, in turn, became the basis for governmental and intergovernmental interest.

The International Labour Office reports that by the time of the London Monetary Conference, in 1933, "Intergovernmental commodity control schemes had come to be regarded as a form of international industrial agreement clearly distinct from, and in many respects preferable to, producers' cartel agreements, especially as a means of regulating the production and

[7] *Analysis of the General Agreement on Tariffs and Trade,* U.S. Department of State Publication 2983, Washington, D.C., 1947, p. 206.

marketing of foodstuffs and raw materials."[8] Wide postwar interest in intergovernmental arrangements stems from activities directed toward expanding international trade by a number of devices and from social objectives given prominence in declarations of the United Nations Charter.

The objectives of such agreements are often described in such terms as "minimizing price fluctuations," "establishing more orderly marketing conditions," "contributing to the expansion rather than the restriction of employment and trade," and "establishing a more orderly adjustment of supply and demand." The postwar concept of intergovernmental arrangements is held out to be constantly alert to the needs for expanding production, trade, and employment and as being opposed to the restrictive practices of producer cartels. In general, this is accomplished by having representation on controlling bodies of both producer and consumer governments, which was not formerly the case.

Governmental interest in commodity arrangements is based substantially on the following considerations: (1) Some commodities are of major interest to the economies of certain countries; (2) international trade in certain primary commodities does not follow the pattern of trade in, say, manufactured goods, because the demand is relatively inelastic (in terms of price), and production adjustments cannot be effected by the free play of market forces as rapidly as the circumstances require; (3) burdensome surpluses are accompanied by widespread distress to small producers, because a substantial reduction in price leads neither to a significant increase in consumption nor to a significant decrease in production; and (4) national measures to relieve hardship caused by low income and unemployment often result in action bearing on other countries—to use a popular term, in exporting their unemployment to other countries. Superimposed on this is the increased direct role of government in the economy (especially with regard to incomes and employment) and the formation of many new countries that formerly were subject to metropolitan powers.

There has been a clamor, also, especially from developing countries, for more regularized international trade in the products which are of special interest to them and which may, in fact, be their principal sources of foreign exchange earnings.

Most of the intergovernmental agreements concern themselves with primary commodities. But interest in intergovernmental arrangements is not exclusive to developing countries. Because of the ability of low-wage countries to produce the same product as does the high-wage, highly industrialized

[8] *Intergovernmental Commodity Control Agreement,* International Labour Office, Montreal, 1943, p. xx.

country, there is intergovernmental interest in controlling the impact of such competition. In one case, that of cotton textiles, an intergovernmental agreement pertaining to international trade in the product has been in force for some years and was extended in 1967 as part of the Kennedy Round negotiations.

Intergovernmental commodity agreements are of several types. An essential characteristic is that they are multilateral in composition and pertain to a specific commodity. In this sense the U.S.-Canadian automotive parts agreement is a trade agreement, but not technically a commodity agreement. Nor would the reciprocal trade agreements negotiated by the United States and many other countries over the past 30 years be called commodity agreements—they deal with a number of products rather than a specific one.

The important point about intergovernmental commodity agreements, for our purpose, is that such agreements do or may regulate international trade in the commodity in question, affecting sources, markets, or prices. By so doing, they determine, or at least influence, the patterns, volumes, and flows of a significant amount of trade as well as terms of trade between trading nations.

Despite several years of intense interest and discussion of the subject, during which time the U.S. position toward such commitments was modified,[9] only a few agreements have actually come into existence—that is, only a few to which the United States is a party or which could truly be called multilateral agreements. These are:

Agreements

International Coffee Agreement (55 countries).

International Sugar Agreement (46 countries). This one was practically inoperative in 1967.

International Wheat Agreement (49 countries).

International Long-Term Cotton Textile Agreement (30 countries).

Study groups

International Cocoa Study Group.

International Hard Fibers Study Group.

International Lead and Zinc Study Group.

[9] In 1961, at the Inter-American Economic and Social Conference, held at Punta del Este, Secretary of the Treasury Dillon advised the other governments that the United States was now prepared to consider favorably proposals for such arrangements on a case-by-case basis, despite years of previous opposition in principle.

International Rubber Study Group.
International Wool Study Group.

There is also an International Olive Oil Agreement and an International Tin Agreement, in neither of which the United States participates. However, private American international business may have to be directly interested in such agreements, even though the U.S. Government itself does not participate.

Chapter VI

Customs Unions, Free Trade Areas, and Other Preferences

Historically, preferential trading arrangements between independent states are not new on the international scene.[1] They have come into increasing prominence in recent decades, however, for several reasons: They run counter to the broader moves toward nondiscriminatory liberalization of trading opportunities; they are condoned by the General Agreement on Tariffs and Trade (GATT); several new ones have been formed in the postwar period; and the breakup of mother country-territorial relationships and the formation of many new countries has created an atmosphere in which newly formed nations seem to feel they need discriminatory measures favoring themselves and perhaps selected others. Older developing countries have also spoken out for preferences favoring them in trading opportunities as a spur to their development. In this sense, they ask for preferential treatment which is not available to their competitors in developed countries.

BENEFITS TO PARTICIPANTS AND FEARS OF OUTSIDERS

The fundamental benefit to participants in a preferential area, when such an institution takes the form of a customs union or a free area, is that

[1] Perhaps the best known until the postwar period was the Zollverein, formed in 1833, which served as a base for unification of Germany in the mid-19th century.

the market for producers within is enlarged. Competition from inside may be increased, while competition from outside is reduced. This is the practical meaning of preferential arrangements to international business. Such preferences may also be, depending on the level of duties, a motivation for businesses outside to come in, via investment or licensing.

In general, those outside preferential areas fear exclusion from previously competitive trading opportunities and that some of their competition, which formerly had to pay the same duties as they, are now to be exempt from the duties. Related to this is the broader consideration of whether formation of a preferential arrangement will have a *trade-creating* or a *trade-diverting* effect. Trade-creating effect, as used here, means that wider geographic markets, with obstacles to trade reduced or eliminated, will: stimulate efficiency through increased competition of an acceptable type; stimulate better allocation of economic resources; stimulate additional investment; and stimulate economic growth. This, in turn, will increase the demand for additional imports and thereby create more trade and have a less harmful effect on countries outside the preference area. Concurrent with this increase in efficiency and productivity will be the likelihood of an increase in exports, thereby also creating more trade. Trade-diverting effect, as used here, means the simple replacement of one supplier, who must continue to pay the price of trade restrictions, by another supplier, who no longer has to because of his situation in the preference area. This may mean diverting business from low-cost producers outside to high-cost producers within.

Not all preferential trading arrangements are customs unions or free trade areas. The Commonwealth preference system is not; members still pay some duties, where they are imposed, but at a lower rate than others. A similar type of preference is that by which the United States legally favors Cuba.[2] Therefore, the advantages to insiders and the disadvantages to outsiders are not as great as would be the case were there no duties or other restrictions within the area.

GATT attitude toward customs unions and free trade areas. The closest that the modern world has come to an agreed and effective code of conduct in international trade relationships is the General Agreement on Tariffs and Trade. In considering the place of preferences in the international business world, the contracting parties to GATT recognized the desirability of increasing freedom of trade by the development, through voluntary agreements, of closer integration among the economies of the countries which are

[2] This provision of the law has been suspended by the Tariff Classification Act of 1962.

parties to such agreements. They also agreed that the purpose of a customs union or of a free trade area should be to facilitate trade among the constituent territories and at the same time *not* to raise barriers to the trade of other contracting parties with such territories.[3]

A customs union was defined as a single customs territory as replacement for two or more customs territories so that duties and other restrictive regulations of commerce would be eliminated with respect to substantially all trade between constituent territories of the union, and that substantially the same duties and other regulations of commerce would be applied by each of the members of the union to the trade of territories not included in the union.[4] This requires the development of a common external tariff. A free trade area was defined as a group of two or more customs territories in which duties and other restrictive regulations of commerce are eliminated on substantially all the trade between the constituent territories in products originating in such territories, but in which the employment of a common external tariff is not required.[5] In addition, GATT authorizes the formation of customs unions or free trade areas provided that the resulting duties and other regulations are not higher or more restrictive than those which existed prior to formation of the preferential area.[6]

Preferences predating GATT. GATT was negotiated in 1947 and came onto the scene after some preferential arrangements had already been in force. It was only to be expected, then, that existing arrangements would not be summarily terminated, for the partners thereto would not have agreed. Instead, exceptions were made for a number of arrangements, such as those between: the Commonwealth countries; metropolitan France and territories of the French Union; Benelux and certain overseas territories related to the metropolitan countries; the United States and the Philippines; the United States and Cuba; and certain neighboring countries. In Article XXIV, however, GATT provided that the margin of preference was not to be increased above that in force as of certain designated dates.

EXISTING AND PROPOSED PREFERENTIAL ARRANGEMENTS

Some preferential arrangements between independent countries are of long standing. Until the last decade they were generally between small and contiguous territories, or between a major country and a smaller one, and

[3] Article XXIV, Paragraph 4.
[4] *Ibid.*, Paragraph 8.
[5] *Ibid.*
[6] *Ibid.*, Paragraph 5.

not between major trading partners. Examples of such arrangements in force for many years are those between Belgium and Luxembourg (1922), France and Monaco (1865), Italy and San Marino (1862), and Switzerland and Liechtenstein (1924). To this should be added the preferences given by the United States to Cuba and the Philippines following their independence. The first of these, as mentioned earlier, has been suspended, and the latter is being phased out.

With the end of World War II, however, the advantages of closer economic ties became apparent, and a wave of new preferences and discriminatory arrangements came onto the scene. Acceptance of the principle of such arrangements, as against a century-old espousal of the principle of nondiscrimination in trading relationships, was formalized in the exceptions to nondiscriminatory provisions of GATT. This factor, in addition to the formation of two large and successful preferential areas and the emergence of many newly independent nations, apparently generated increased interest in additional discriminatory arrangements to support economic integration and development.

The two outstanding preferential trading areas, if one judges by the importance of their members in world trade, are the European Economic Community (EEC)—its customs union commonly referred to as the Common Market—and the European Free Trade Association (EFTA).

European Economic Community. The treaty establishing the European Economic Community was negotiated in Rome in 1957 among Belgium, Luxembourg, France, the Federal Republic of Germany, Italy, and the Netherlands. EEC goes far beyond its function as a customs union in its direction of complete economic integration. The customs union section of the treaty provided for the scheduled elimination, by stages, of duties and other restrictions, including quantitative restrictions to trade between members; it also provided for the establishment of a common external tariff (CXT) to apply against imports from suppliers outside the community. Accomplishment of CXT was to take place in stages to allow national duties to be adjusted to the CXT level. CXT was, in principle, a weighted average of the individual national tariff rates in force prior to formation of the customs union. Progress toward elimination of internal trading barriers and establishment of CXT was more rapid than had been anticipated, with the result that both features were achieved by July 1968—some 18 months ahead of the original schedule.

By its title, European Economic Community, the broader implications and requirements of economic integration are evident. They include, among other things, a common agricultural policy; provision for the free movement of persons, services, and capital within the territory; a common transport policy; common rules governing competition and fiscal provisions; and closely coordinated, if not common, policies relating to economic trends, balances of payment, and commercial policy. Thus not only were the markets opened in favor of each other, the conditions of competition were also considered and were made more harmonious. The EEC treaty also provides, in Article 237, that any European state may apply to become a member of the Community. Article 238 of the treaty specifies that the Community may conclude with a nonmember country, a union of states, or an international organization, agreements creating an association embodying reciprocal rights and obligations, joint actions, and special procedures. As of mid-1968, associate member status had been negotiated with Greece and Turkey. A number of other European countries have attempted to negotiate special arrangements with EEC, but as of mid-1968 none had been concluded.

European Free Trade Association. Developing substantially at the same time as the European Economic Community was the European Free Trade Association, the principal organizer of which was the United Kingdom. EFTA was established in the Stockholm Convention of 1960 by the United Kingdom, Denmark, Norway, Sweden, Austria, Switzerland, and Portugal. Finland became an associate member in 1961.

The objectives of EFTA were more limited than those of the customs union of EEC. EFTA sought internal free trade in *industrial* products. There was to be no common external tariff, each nation retaining its own national tariff. This appeared to be necessary to the United Kingdom because of its special relationships and responsibilities toward the Commonwealth countries. There was to be no common agricultural policy, and no close harmonization of economic policies such as was undertaken by EEC as a means of more complete economic integration. EFTA achieved its goal of internal free trade at the end of 1967.

The future of EFTA is cloudy, because several of its members have applied for membership in EEC. Their admittance would seem to render EFTA no longer necessary as a separate international economic organization.

Commonwealth preference. This arrangement was negotiated in 1932 in Ottawa. Under it, participating countries agreed to reduce but not eliminate duties among members. Outside countries were not given most-favored-nation treatment.

The margin of preference enjoyed by the United Kingdom in its Commonwealth markets was estimated to be about 12 percent of import value exclusive of duty, and 6.5–7 percent on all imports from the United Kingdom, based on 1961 trade.[7] A comparable study, on the margin of preference on dutiable imports entering the United Kingdom in 1962, shows that about three-fifths of its imports from the Commonwealth enjoyed tariff preference; the average margin of preference on dutiable imports was just under 12 percent of value exclusive of duty, and just over 7 percent of the value of all imports.[8]

Central American Common Market. This preferential arrangement, which qualifies as a customs union under GATT definition, dates from a series of treaties and protocols entered into in the period 1958–60. Member countries are Costa Rica, El Salvador, Guatemala, Honduras, and Nicaragua. This common market has achieved practically complete elimination of duties within the group and full equalization of import duties applied against outsiders. It must therefore be considered a very advanced undertaking.

Latin American Free Trade Association. The treaty establishing this association was signed at Montevideo in 1961. Its original members were Argentina, Brazil, Chile, Mexico, Paraguay, Peru, and Uruguay. These were later joined by Colombia, Ecuador, Venezuela, and Bolivia. Its progress toward free internal trade has been slow. Discussions in the mid-1960's have centered on speeding up the process of liberalizing trade and, more daringly, on the formation of a larger Latin American common market.

New Zealand–Australian Free Trade Area. This association, NAFTA, was formed in 1966. It involves goods moving between New Zealand and Australia only and provides for a phasing out by 1974 of duties on the basis of annual review.

Caribbean Free Trade Association. Ratification was completed in 1966 of the agreement negotiated among Antigua, Barbados, and Guyana to establish this organization, CARIFTA. The accord provides for the eventual elimination of duties and quotas among members and for the harmonization of investment policies. The association became operational in May 1968. Subsequent to this, other British-speaking countries in the Caribbean joined the association, which now includes all such areas except British Honduras and the Bahamas.

Arab Common Market. By 1967 import duties on trade among participating countries in goods covered by the agreement forming the group had been reduced by 60 percent for agricultural goods and 30 percent for industrial goods. Countries making up this market are Iraq, Jordan, the Syrian Arab Republic, and the United Arab Republic.[9]

[7] *Board of Trade Journal,* London, June 11, 1965, p. vii.
[8] *Ibid.,* December 31, 1965, p. 1553.
[9] *Ibid.,* p. 12.

The Council for Mutual Economic Assistance. This organization, COMECON, was established in 1949 by Bulgaria, Czechoslovakia, Hungary, Poland, Rumania, and the Union of Soviet Socialist Republics. East Germany joined in the fall of 1950, and Yugoslavia became an affiliate in 1964. While not a preferential area in the true sense, since trade is carried on by state-owned entities and duties are of no practical consequence because the government would be taxing itself by imposing them, COMECON is included among such arrangements because it has objectives similar to customs unions and free trade areas—that is, it assists in economic development and unification and facilitates the clearing of payments between members.

Various African preferential areas. Africa, having been fragmented by the formation of some 30 to 35 new countries in the postwar period, is the scene of several preferential areas, principally in the planning or "agreed" stages. All of the countries would qualify as underdeveloped; in many, industry is not important, so they do not have much to trade with each other at a given time. But economic development aspirations call for union and cooperation of several types, and a frequent objective is customs unions among various groupings of countries. Among these are:

1. Organization of African Unity. This is the largest of the several groups in membership, with 35 countries. It has requested United Nations assistance in studying the establishment of an African common market with a joint external tariff. The organization dates from 1963.
2. Afro-Malagasy Economic Union. This organization, dating from 1958, is the second largest in membership, with 12 nations, all of which are also members of the Organization of African Unity. Its objectives include economic integration and the creation of a common market.
3. The Casablanca Group. The members of this group (Algeria, Ghana, Guinea, Mali, Morocco, and the United Arab Republic) agreed in 1963 to establish an African common market which would incorporate the establishment of a customs union. As of mid-1968, however, the common market project had not evolved, since the treaty had not been ratified by all signatory countries.
4. West African Customs Union. This union consists of Dahomey, Ivory Coast, Mali, Mauritania, Niger, Senegal, Upper Volta, and Togo. These countries are also members of the Afro-Malagasy Economic Union. They formed a customs union in 1959

(Togo joined in 1966) with the objective of achieving free trade among themselves and harmonizing customs procedures and taxation. Within this customs union a smaller Council of Entente has been formed, consisting of Dahomey, Ivory Coast, Niger, Togo, and Upper Volta.

5. Central African Economic and Customs Union. Four of the members of this organization—Central African Republic, Chad, Congo (Brazzaville), and Gabon—established an Equatorial Customs Union in 1959, and in 1964 these four countries and Cameroon signed an agreement to establish the Central African Economic and Customs Union, which came into being in 1966.
6. East African Common Market. Kenya, Tanzania, and Uganda, all formerly under British control, signed a treaty in 1967 to establish an East African common market. The treaty formalized an existing common external tariff. Under terms of the treaty, internal tariffs are prohibited except under stated conditions.

Other groupings in Africa that have objectives similar to the customs unions and free trade areas previously listed are the Maghreb Economic Community (Algeria, Libya, Morocco, and Tunisia) and a proposed Guinea-Liberia-Sierra Leone-Ivory Coast free trade area. Many of the foregoing are of no great economic significance, worldwide, but their formation points to a wider interest in discriminatory groupings. The fact that many of these countries are not contracting parties to GATT removes the direct influence of the GATT forum, and there is nothing much to prevent their practicing discrimination against outsiders either in favor of former mother countries, of EEC, or of anyone else.

As can be seen, no effort was made to probe into the details of any of these organizations for such information is readily available elsewhere. Obviously, several of the groupings are in the early stages of slow development and face the probability of amendment or modifications in goals, schedules (if any), and membership.

EFFECT ON NONAFFILIATED COUNTRIES

The cry of businesses outside preferential trading arrangements is that someone else is being given an advantage in what was to them a competitive trading opportunity and that they are disadvantaged by it. But the concept of preferential trading arrangements under specified situations and as a means of fostering economic integration has been accepted by GATT. Therefore, in order to rectify the unfavorable effect on themselves, countries outside preferential trading arrangements are left with one of two choices: join on some basis with the preferential arrangement of most significance to them, or negotiate to have the degrees of preference afforded other countries reduced. Evolution of the preferential arrangements we have reviewed has stimulated efforts in these directions.

Impact on the United States. From our earliest days as a nation, our commercial policy objective has been to obtain equal treatment in doing business with independent countries. We have eschewed seeking discriminatory benefits for ourselves. It has been our policy, also, to grant equal treatment to all except those discriminating against our commerce. The result was the achievement of a practical, nondiscriminatory trading world until the depression of the 1930's.

But with the United States not involved in any of the preferential arrangements just described, one must wonder what the effect has been or will be on U.S. export trade. Hopefully, the trade-creating characteristics of common markets and free trade areas embracing important export markets and enclosing important competitors for those markets will more than offset the trade-diversion characteristics.

That this is quite possible was demonstrated by one investigation of U.S. performance as a competitor in EEC after its preferences began to be significant. It was found that not only did the dollar value of imports from the United States increase as compared with its position prior to formation of the Common Market, but the U.S. *share* of the market was substantially retained and in a number of cases increased.[10]

Aside from any quantitative indication of the impact on the United States of the formation of preferential trading arrangements, a recent survey showed that, although the United States has treaties or other international agreements calling for nondiscriminatory treatment for American products with respect to customs duties in 102 countries, many of these countries do not, in fact, grant such treatment because of agreed derogations therefrom. In all of the important foreign markets (those taking more than 1 percent of U.S. exports), except Japan and Venezuela, U.S. exporters of products dutiable abroad face competition that is in a preferred position with respect to duties.[11] Approximately 80 percent of all American exports go to markets

[10] Harold J. Heck, "The United States as a Competitor in the EEC Import Market," *Columbia Journal of World Business,* September–October 1967, pp. 47–52.

[11] *The Most-Favored-Nation Principle,* Chamber of Commerce of the United States, Washington, D.C., 1966, p. 13.

in which other suppliers, in some cases our strongest competitors, enjoy preferences with respect to import duties.[12]

Influence on former overseas territories. One cannot overlook the fact that former overseas territories of the European countries making up EEC were closely tied to and dependent on them. It would be impractical to expect these former dependencies, upon achieving independence, to suddenly break away and make their own way economically, politically, and socially. Therefore, something had to be done to preserve the institutions by which they lived. This was done by offering them the opportunity for associate status in EEC.

The EEC members had agreed in Article 131 of the Rome Treaty to bring into association with the Community the non-European countries and territories that had special relations with France, Belgium, Italy, and the Netherlands. But within a few years, many of these had become independent countries. Upon achieving independence, they were invited to renegotiate the association on a basis of equality; all of the countries concerned except Guinea accepted the offer.

The primary broad arrangement for associating independent African countries with EEC is the Yaoundé Convention, which became effective in June 1964. Signatories were the EEC countries and 18 African countries; the Netherlands Antilles and Surinam have since associated themselves with EEC. There is nothing in the convention to prevent the associated states' favoring EEC suppliers over outsiders; this concerns countries outside EEC. By EEC council decision, association is also provided for the overseas territories of French Polynesia, St. Pierre and Miquelon, and New Caledonia. Thus the preferential benefits that EEC members give each other are now extended to new countries as well as to remaining dependencies of EEC members. The preferential area has *widened.*

EEC member states approved a declaration of intent at the time of the signing of the Yaoundé Convention which left the door open for accession on the part of other African states with economies similar to and production comparable to those of the Yaoundé associates. These other African states were to be permitted to accede to the Yaoundé Convention, apply for a separate association, or negotiate a trade agreement covering selected products. Principal among the countries involved here are Nigeria and the East African states of Kenya, Tanzania, and Uganda, all of which have British Commonwealth backgrounds, and Algeria, Morocco, and Tunisia. An agreement was reached which associated Nigeria with EEC in 1966, whereby Nigeria accorded to the Community small customs preferences on 26 commodities. The Community agreed to allow all but four Nigerian exports to enter at

[12] *Ibid.,* pp. 13–14.

the internal rates of duty. As of mid-1968, conversations concerning future economic relations were under way between EEC and Algeria, Morocco, and Tunisia. Difficulties were being encountered, however, because the burden of granting useful concessions would fall heavily on Italy, and because Algeria was already receiving special treatment from France and Germany. One of the complications is that no one starts from scratch; he is faced with a number of entrenched positions or privileges.

Trade involving EEC members and neighbors. Because of proximity to EEC, or to one or more of its members, other countries over the years have developed trading ties with countries now in EEC. Moreover, because of the geographic coverage of EEC and the industrial and agricultural resources of its members, many European nonmembers have faced a potentially significant loss of markets to the now-favored producers within EEC. In this category are some of the Mediterranean countries facing competition from production within Italy and southern France. They are, in addition, confronted by development of the productive capacities of EEC—which is, indeed, one of its objectives. The situation has been particularly acute for some countries that had been selling a large part of their exports into EEC, and which were not in a favorable position to seek world markets elsewhere because of small size and the distance from other markets. For example, about 45 percent of Austria's total exports went to EEC in 1966,[13] as did 38 percent of Switzerland's and 30 percent of Sweden's. Twenty-seven percent of Austria's total, 15 percent of Switzerland's, and 13 percent of Sweden's went to Germany. Other countries with a high percentage of their total exports going to EEC were (in 1964) : Turkey, 35 percent; Greece, 35 percent; and Spain, 33 percent. It is obvious that these are overall statistics that do not reveal pressure points. Some of the trade moves at very low duty or no duty and would only be threatened by increased production within EEC; another part will be concentrated much more heavily in one product than in another; this is not disclosed by the averages. But fears and potential injuries exist by sector, industry, and product.

In view of these circumstances, and their desire to join in the political evolution surrounding the Common Market, some European countries not in EEC began promptly to investigate the possibility of membership in or association with EEC. The first of these nations was Greece, which applied for associate status in June 1959. Agreement was reached in November 1962 under which Greece was admitted as an associate member; full membership will be granted after a transition period of 22 years if her economy permits the assumption of all the obligations of the Rome treaty. Turkey

[13] *EFTA Trade* (1959–66), European Free Trade Association, Geneva, January 1968, p. 16.

applied for associate membership in July 1959 and was admitted as such in September 1963. The understanding here is that Turkey will be considered for full membership when her economy permits the assumption of all obligations of the Rome Treaty. Spain applied in 1962 for associate status with a view to full membership in due course, but as of 1968 it had not been determined that this eventual goal would be attainable or mutually desirable. Yugoslavia has also expressed interest in an agreement with EEC, and a study initiated in 1967 is exploring terms of a possible nondiscriminatory trading agreement between EEC and that country.[14]

There was considerable opposition to EEC in its formative stages in the late 1950's by countries unable or unwilling to accept some of its obligations, but which had no desire to be economically or politically disadvantaged. The ultimate result was the formation, in January 1960, of EFTA, a parallel trading organization. In time, Great Britain, finding itself unable to arrest EEC's growth, attempted to negotiate a satisfactory working relationship with it on behalf of itself and its EFTA partners. Within a few months of the British application, Ireland, Denmark, and Norway had applied for membership, and Austria, Sweden, Switzerland, and Portugal had applied for associate status. When circumstances caused the termination of negotiations with Great Britain, however, the applications of the other EFTA countries and Ireland were suspended, and no serious negotiations took place. In May 1967 the British Government resumed its effort by applying for full membership under Article 237 of the Rome Treaty. In doing so, Britain indicated its readiness to accept all three treaties comprising the European Economic Community[15] ". . . subject only to adjustments required to provide for the accession of a new member. . . ." A big hurdle was overcome, obviously, in Britain's indicated willingness to accept EEC's common agricultural policy, and resolution of its Commonwealth responsibilities appeared within grasp. Some opposition to absorbing Britain into EEC was evident, however, in the French Foreign Minister's statement that ". . . admission of Britain and some of her EFTA partners would destroy the Communities as they now exist and bring about a much larger, more ineffective, and more amorphous free trade grouping."[16] By mid-1968, no progress had been made on even the beginning of negotiations.

Trade agreements. Still another way in which nonmembers of preferential trading groups may act to protect themselves against the burden of

[14] *Informational Memo* (Summary of Xth General Report of the Commission), European Economic Community, Brussels, June 1967.

[15] These treaties encompass the Common Market, European Coal and Steel Community, and Euratom.

[16] *European Free Trade Association Reporter,* European Free Trade Association, Washington, D.C., July 17, 1967, p. 1.

preferences is by negotiating for special or defensive treatment for one or many products, in the form of an agreement designed to expand trade between the nonmember and the preference group. EEC has concluded agreements of this type with Israel and Iran. These agreements are nondiscriminatory; therefore, the duty reductions apply to imports of these products from other sources as well. By the selection of products, however, the agreements are designed mainly to benefit Iran and Israel. A trade agreement with Lebanon, in which most-favored-nation status is mutually conceded, also includes an undertaking for rendering technical assistance to Lebanon.

Reduction of preferential benefits. The reason for support of the concept of preferential trading arrangements, by members and nonmembers alike, is that the potential advantages are not only economic; they are political as well, and in some cases primarily so. Economic integration is thus a means to an end, and some countries and businesses stand to pay a stiff price for attaining this economic objective. Typically, however, preferential trading arrangements are between countries, and cover many, if not most, products.[17] Another reason for support of the broad concept of preferential benefits is that trade agreements among the major trading nations are usually broad—that is, they are not typically barter arrangements nor do they specify a certain volume of trade in relatively few products. In light of these two characteristics of most preferential trading arrangements, one can better understand and accept the attitude of the major nations toward such arrangements.

Again, the experience of EEC is revealing. By GATT rules, the incidence of duties of a customs union, which EEC is, must not be higher than it was prior to formation of the union. Because of the interest of several "outside" countries in not being disadvantaged on a broad scale, the EEC authorities took several significant steps to soften the blow of their preferences to each other. First, after the common external tariff was negotiated between EEC members, it was provisionally reduced by 20 percent as a target for negotiation in the Dillon Round of GATT negotiations concluded in 1962. At that time, however, the preferences had not really begun to take hold, as the timetable did not call for much of a reduction at first. Then, when the first 10 percent reduction in duties was to be made in favor of other EEC partners, the 10 percent reduction was "generalized," that is, passed on to other countries of GATT which were not members of EEC.[18]

[17] An exception is the automobile parts agreement between the United States and Canada.

[18] *The Common Market,* European Community Information Service, Brussels, September 1961.

The main move toward a negotiated reduction of preferences did not, however, take place until passage of the Trade Expansion Act of 1962 by the U.S. Congress. Under this authority, negotiations were held under GATT auspices in what has come to be known as the Kennedy Round, concluded in 1967. One must look on this achievement not only as a reduction in rates of duty for any given product or list of products, but as a reduction in the level of preferences, generally. EEC, which has a common external tariff, negotiated as a unit. Members of EFTA, which maintain national tariffs, participated individually, as did Japan and the United States. It is estimated that over 50 countries participated in one form or another.[19]

Prior to the Kennedy Round negotiations, EEC's common external tariff averaged about 11.7 percent *ad valorem,* as against 17.9 percent for the United States and 18.4 percent for the British tariff.[20] On industrial products, the major trading partners agreed on reductions in duties averaging about 35 percent over a five-year period. In agriculture the average cut was less, but important concessions of other types were obtained.[21]

[19] *International Commerce,* U.S. Department of Commerce, Washington, D.C., July 31, 1967, p. 2.

[20] *European Community, The Facts,* European Community Information Office, Washington, D.C., August 1967, p. 28.

[21] *Summary of the Kennedy Round Package,* prepared for National Conference on the Kennedy Round, sponsored by Chamber of Commerce of the United States, Washington, D.C., July 7, 1967.

Chapter VII

Export Expansion and Restrictions

It should be no surprise that, companion to the opening of foreign market opportunities through negotiation, most governments offer special aids to exporters of products originating in their territories. The types of aid vary widely, but their existence testifies to the importance of exports as a means of absorbing production, as a foundation for jobs arising from production and servicing of exports, and as a source of foreign exchange which can be used to pay for imports. Related to the latter is a justification for such aids in terms of balance of payments considerations.

In some cases, governments offer incentives directly to exporters; in others, only indirect assistance is provided. Examples of the former are tax rebates, tax reductions or exemptions, and direct financial assistance. Examples of the latter are promotional services, the gathering and dissemination of commercial intelligence and trading opportunities, and special programs, such as encouragement and assistance in participation in trade fairs, trade missions, and the like.

TAX AND FINANCIAL INCENTIVES

A popular device for direct stimulation of exports is the use of the taxing mechanism, either through tax rebates or through the allowance of charges that reduce income subject to tax. The two most widely used tax rebate arrangements appear to be drawbacks of import duties paid on goods subsequently exported and the refund of indirect taxes, such as sales, excise, or turnover taxes, paid to the government prior to export, or excluded from application on sales destined for export.

The practice of rebating taxes as an incentive to exports has drawn public attention in the United States in recent years, with the underlying thought that perhaps part of the income tax—that part attributable to income from export sales—might be rebated. It is claimed that U.S. exporters are disadvantaged because of the inability of the United States to rebate income tax, while exporters in other countries, whose governments make wider use of indirect taxing methods, are favored by their governments, which are able to and do refund or exempt some of these taxes.[1]

The General Agreement on Tariffs and Trade appears to approve of the refund only of taxes *borne by the product* when destined for consumption in a country other than that of origin or exportation, and by inference to disallow the rebate of taxes on *income* arising from export sales (which taxes are "direct" and not borne by a given product). The GATT document, itself, does not specifically prohibit the rebate of taxes on income attributable to exports. But a rather positive stand against export subsidies is taken in Article XVI, Section B. Subsequent to this, in 1960, a Working Party Report intending to give effect to Article XVI's provisions listed a number of measures which, in the view of those countries signing the declaration, would be considered as export subsidies and therefore contrary to GATT. Among these is (Item C), "the remission, calculated in relation to exports, of direct taxes or social welfare charges on industrial and commercial enterprises." The United States was one of the signers of this declaration, along with some 16 other industrial countries. Therefore, the rebate of income taxes as an export incentive could not well be authorized by the United States. However, a number of developing GATT countries and, of course, the non-GATT countries did not sign the declaration and therefore have not adopted the position that such a rebate is a subsidy. Yet the practice of rebating taxes on income earned from exports does not appear to be widespread.

Among the special allowable charges against income which serve to stimulate exports are:

- Deduction, as an expense in computing taxable income, of an amount exceeding actual expenses for export promotion.

[1] See, for example, Richard W. Lindholm, "Tax Disharmony: A Basic Cause of International Payments Imbalance," *Michigan Business Review,* November 1965, p. 17.

- Extra depreciation allowances on a formula relating overseas transactions to total business.
- Establishment of reserves, free of tax, for reinvestment within a certain time period in overseas market development or in "export assets."

An even more direct export expansion incentive is the provision of financial assistance which may be available in advance and without particular reference to profitability of the venture. Among recent facilities of this type were special or preferential credit terms in favor of companies exporting, say, specified percentages of sales, or specified minimum amounts, and direct subsidies, which have been employed in several countries, including the United States, but which are not widely used.

SPECIAL AGRICULTURAL EXPORT PROGRAMS

In addition to the incentives just mentioned, which are not related to the exportation of any given product, direct incentives are found that are intended primarily or only to increase the exportation of certain products or types of products. An outstanding example of these pertains to the export of agricultural products by the United States.

Public Law 480. Agricultural products have long been and remain among the most important of U.S. export groups. In fact, several agricultural commodities are among the leading export products. However, production in the United States of some commodities had been so great that domestic and foreign consumption through normal marketing operations was unable to clear the market; the result was a surplus of certain agricultural commodities in the disposal of which special programs have been undertaken.

The major arrangement of this type is Public Law 480 (68 Stat. 454), originally passed in 1954 and since extended and amended. This law, cited as the Agricultural Trade Development and Assistance Act, seeks to overcome the difficulty of selling abroad under normal short-term dollar terms. This is done primarily by (1) private sales for nonconvertible foreign currencies, which are then sold by American exporters to the U.S. Government for dollars, and (2) arranging long-term supply contracts under which foreign sales for domestic consumption during periods of economic development are made for U.S. dollars, on long-term credit. Under the law sales may also be made on a barter basis, and certain donations are authorized.

In all cases arrangements are negotiated with the foreign government concerned. Care is taken to insure that the disposals do not displace U.S. cash dollar sales or disrupt normal patterns of commercial trade among friendly countries, and that maximum use is made of private trade channels.

When the United States comes into possession of foreign nonconvertible currencies, their use must be legally authorized, and this must be consonant with the desires of the host country. The uses authorized by the Congress, limitations on which may be insisted on by the host country during the negotiation, are several, including: (1) payment of U.S. obligations and carrying out government programs, such as developing new markets for agricultural commodities and financing international educational and cultural activities, (2) loans to private business firms, (3) promoting economic development, and (4) sales to U.S. citizens for travel and other purposes.

CCC export credit sales program. In addition to the arrangement for encouraging agricultural disposal abroad via Public Law 480, the Department of Agriculture's Commodity Credit Corporation (CCC) has established an Export Credit Sales Program, which is designed to boost commercial farm exports for dollars. The program began in February 1966. It functions by the CCC's issuing export commodity certificates to U.S. exporters of specified commodities sold to buyers in designated countries within permissible credit time limits. These certificates may be used to obtain commodities from CCC-owned stocks to fill export orders, or the export sale may be supplied from privately owned stocks, which may then be replenished by redeeming the certificates with the CCC.

The maximum permissible credit limit is three years, although the general policy is to limit the terms to twelve months for cotton, grain sorghums, and tobacco, and to six months for all other commodities. With respect to these time limits, the exporter makes his sale and requires the foreign buyer to arrange for a bank letter of credit in favor of the CCC, providing for payment in U.S. dollars. What the program does is to make it possible for an American exporter to sell abroad on more liberal credit terms (as far as time is concerned), provided the sale is covered with an irrevocable letter of credit in favor of the Commodity Credit Corporation.

FOREIGN CREDIT INSURANCE ASSOCIATION (FCIA)

The FCIA is an unincorporated association, or a syndicate, of some 65 private insurance companies which, in cooperation with the Export-Import Bank, insures trade credits granted by U.S. exporters to buyers in all friendly countries. Through this joint arrangement (private and government), insurance is available to the exporter against loss resulting from commercial credit risks and/or political risks. The FCIA assumes the liability for commercial credit losses, subject to an aggregate loss limit of $2.5 million annually. The Export-Import Bank assumes the liability for political risks and reinsures the FCIA for risks in excess of $150,000 per buyer and for losses in excess of FCIA's aggregate annual loss limit of $2.5 million.

The *commericial credit risks* with which the FCIA is concerned are those of the buyer's insolvency or his protracted payment default. The *political risks* are primarily those such as government actions which block or delay transfer of the buyer's local currency payment, in dollars, to the exporter; or the cancellation of export or import licenses under circumstances not due to the fault of the buyer; or the imposition of any law or regulation which, under circumstances that are not the fault of the buyer, prevents the import of such shipment into the buyer's country.

Initially, FCIA export credit insurance did not apply to shipments sold for any currency other than U.S. dollars, but in early 1966 this requirement was modified to provide cover for short-term credit sales denominated in foreign currencies—but not to the extent of covering the exchange risk.

The types of policies available are short- and medium-term comprehensive, and short- and medium-term political. The percentages of risk that may normally be insured under each are as follows:

Type of Policy	*Political Risks*	*Commercial Risks*
Short-term comprehensive	95%	90%
Short-term political	90%	
Medium-term comprehensive	90%	90%
Medium-term political	90%	

Under either of the short-term coverages, the exporter must insure all eligible shipments to all markets sold on such credit terms, with certain exceptions. These are shipments to Canada; those paid for in advance or under irrevocable letter of credit; and sales to branches, subsidiaries, and other affiliates, provided the remaining business represents an acceptable volume and spread of market risks for the insurer. Coverage of medium-term credits is available on a case-by-case basis, with no requirement that the exporter cover all his medium-term transactions. Ever since its inception, the export credit insurance program that is available to U.S. exporters has been criticized for its shortcomings (mainly in the eyes of some exporters), and its coverage has been broadened and diversified to increase its appeal to potential participants.

It is estimated that around 2 percent of annual American exports are covered by credit insurance. By comparison, 27 percent of Britain's annual exports are insured, while in France the comparable figure is 20 percent; in Germany it is 7 to 10 percent; and in Canada the estimate is over 60 percent of that country's insurable exports (sales on credit terms to countries other than the United States).[2]

The low percentage of U.S. exports covered by credit insurance, as compared with the experience of several other countries, was referred to by Harold F. Linder, president of the Export-Import Bank, in an address given at the annual meeting of the Banker's Association for Foreign Trade in Boca Raton, Florida, on April 26, 1966. He made the point that such a single percentage does not take account of many differences in the economies and trading patterns of the United States and the other trading nations; for example:

- A sizable portion of U.S. exports is shipped under AID, Department of Agriculture, or Department of Defense arrangements and therefore does not call for export credit insurance.
- Bulk commodities make up an unusually large share of U.S. exports; many of these sales are for cash or on such short terms as to require no insurance.
- A significant share of our exports is shipped by U.S. companies to their foreign subsidiaries and affiliates, and therefore credit insurance is not normally needed (*Survey of Current Business,* December 1965, reports that about 25 percent of U.S. commercial exports are to affiliates of U.S. companies).
- Many U.S. corporations are larger and more soundly financed than are their overseas competitors; they are thus better able to be self-insurers of their export credits.
- Under the U.S. program, exporters have the option of excluding shipments to Canada from required short-term coverage, and Canada is the biggest export market for the United States.

International coordination of credit insurance. As with private companies competing for sales, where there is always the pressure to meet and beat competition—either on price or on credit terms—the governmental or quasi-governmental credit insurance facilities are similarly under pressure to help exporters obtain sales. Thus there is the danger of a credit race with terms

[2] Francis X. Scafuro, *The World's Principal Export Credit Insurance Systems,* International Export Credits Institute, New York, 1967.

more liberal than justified by the competitive private market. Hence the national credit insurance programs found it advisable to associate internationally in order to accomplish certain objectives, among which were standardizing of policy provisions and the holding of payment terms within reasonable limits.

The first of these, the International Credit Insurance Association (ICIA) of Zurich, Switzerland, was founded in 1928. Its membership of some 20 companies in 18 countries consists principally of private insurers who underwrite commercial credit risks, both domestic and export. The second is the *Union d'Assurers des Crédits Internationaux,* better known as the Berne Union, with headquarters at Berne, Switzerland, and a secretariat in Paris. The Berne Union members are mainly government-owned or -supported export credit insurers who underwrite political risks as well as (in most cases) commercial risks. This union was founded in 1934, and membership consists of some 26 insurers in 20 countries. Both the FCIA and the Export-Import Bank of Washington are Berne Union members.

Berne Union members observe a nonbinding "gentlemen's agreement" to avoid excess international competition in credit terms. Generally speaking, its members agree to confine all their underwriting of medium-term credits, granted to buyers of capital goods and so on, to five years after delivery, except for certain types of jet aircraft or ships for which terms of seven years after delivery may be allowed. Members agree to notify the union of departures from the adopted credit limits, thus permitting the competing exporters in other member countries to relax on credit terms on which prior thereto there had been some agreement.[3] Membership in the Berne Union includes all major industrial exporters in the free world except Japan.

THE FOREIGN SERVICE OF THE UNITED STATES

It is as a facility in export expansion that the Foreign Service of the United States is now mentioned, because it is the arm of the U.S. Government that collects and reports virtually all commercial and economic intelligence on foreign markets for the benefit of American business. True, the intelligence on foreign markets so collected is dispensed at retail by the Department of Commerce, which operates a network of field offices in major cities over the country, but the origin is the network of economic and commercial officers located in our embassies and consulates abroad.

[3] Stanley E. Hollis, *Guide to Export Credit Insurance,* Third (Revised) Edition, Foreign Credit Insurance Association, New York, 1966.

The key officer in this facility is the commercial attaché (or commercial counselor in some embassies), who is administratively part of the economic section of the embassy. He is the point of contact for visiting businessmen and has the prime responsibility of being alert to impediments and obstacles to American commerce abroad and of seeking out opportunities for American exports and investments or licensing. Information is also gathered on import opportunities, but these are relatively less emphasized.

Types of commercial reporting. The devices most commonly used in the provision of intelligence on foreign markets are:

1. Reports and observations (in prose and not necessarily standardized). The reports may be scheduled, specifically requested, or voluntary. These, most of which are unclassified, are made available to the public on a loan basis and are sometimes reproduced for the public.
2. Trade Lists. These are "industry" lists of firms engaged in specified types of activity. While collected on a country basis, they are arranged primarily by product, then by the nature of activity surrounding the product: manufacturers, importers, wholesalers, dealers, retailers, and so on, or a combination of these. The lists indicate whether each firm is small, medium, or large, and each name included in the list is supported by specific credit type of intelligence on the firm; this additional intelligence is available in companion reports called *World Trade Directory Reports.* The trade lists do not themselves indicate whether the firms named are presently doing business with U.S. firms. Neither do they specify whether the firm is interested in doing so. But one may safely infer that each listed firm is so interested, for the detailed information on the firm needed for the *World Trade Directory Reports,* which backstops the Trade Lists, is voluntarily given, and its purpose is known.
3. *World Trade Directory Reports.* As mentioned above, these are modest credit-information types of reports, prepared on individual firms abroad by the Foreign Service. They give such information as: names of principal officers and directors, capitalization, antecedents of firm, nature of activity, size (number of salesmen and territory in which active), bank references, names of foreign firms with which business relations have been established.
4. Trade contact surveys. In addition to the simple task of provid-

ing names and information on them, commercial officers of the Foreign Service are also prepared to undertake, for a modest fee paid to the Department of Commerce, a trade contact survey. This involves bringing an American firm's export interest to the attention of a selected number of foreign firms, which are then interviewed to determine whether they would be interested in representing the American firm. The Foreign Service does not select the successful foreign firm, itself, but does submit three final names to the American firm, with supporting data. The American firm can then make its own selection, after making any additional investigation it wishes.

5. Trade opportunities and investment opportunities. Commercial officers of the Foreign Service are on the alert for trade opportunities, and this fact is made known to foreign business groups, such as chambers of commerce or trade associations. As a result, as opportunities are uncovered, the fact is reported to Washington for dissemination to the business community. This is done primarily by publication in *International Commerce* and by reference to appropriate export-minded organizations, which then bring them to the attention of their members.
6. Assistance to trade missions and assistance in participation in trade fairs. While promotional and organizational work in connection with trade missions and trade fairs abroad is done in the United States by the Department of Commerce, the facilities of the Foreign Service are called on for working with them while overseas. This is accomplished by suggesting and arranging itineraries and schedules for missions, by accompanying them, and by reporting on the significance and effectiveness of the trade fairs that are important marketing institutions in many countries of the world.

FOREIGN AGRICULTURAL SERVICE

The Foreign Agricultural Service is administratively and functionally part of the Department of Agriculture and not of the Department of State or the Foreign Service of the United States. Agricultural attachés are posted in about 60 important foreign markets, and these officers are charged with reporting on crop conditions, on primary commodity markets, and with finding and assisting in the development of export opportunities for American agricultural products.

EXPORT PROMOTION AND ASSISTANCE (DEPARTMENT OF COMMERCE)

Far more varied than export incentives are the several types of export assistance offered by governments to their business communities. The type and extent of such assistance are influenced by the degree to which governments control or participate actively in their economies, by the importance of foreign trade to their economies, and by the structure of the export sector of the economy. Practically every country attempts to promote or assist its exports through a foreign commercial service. In some, as in the cases of the United States and the United Kingdom, the overseas commercial service is an integral part of the diplomatic representation; in others, it is a separate service (the Foreign Agricultural Service of the United States and certain overseas activities of the Departments of Commerce and of Interior fit into the latter group), as these functions are not officially part of the Foreign Service of the United States. Export promotion and assistance in the United States is the responsibility of the Department of Commerce, which is organized on a commodity and geographic basis and which coordinates its promotional activity through a very active Office of International Trade Promotion.

Among the indirect types of assistance or activities in which governments participate, more or less, are:

1. Selecting products and markets on which to expend effort and funds toward export promotion.
2. Negotiating trade agreements with foreign countries.
3. Conducting or sponsoring technological research to improve quality of production and adaptation to foreign requirements or demands.
4. Collecting and making information available on international standards.
5. Collecting and making available information on world markets and their requirements. Related to this is information on documentation, tariffs, and customs regulations.
6. Placing producers and exporters in contact with prospective buyers abroad, such buyers either being prescreened or not.
7. Collecting information on trade opportunities and publicizing inquiries received from abroad.
8. Organizing participation in international trade fairs and exhibitions and in special promotional activities.
9. Establishing and operating trade commissioner offices and showrooms in important foreign market centers.

10. Subsidizing shipping facilities to encourage direct and frequent services, and to avoid the delay and expense of transhipment, thereby reducing transportation costs and improving service.

RESTRICTIONS ON OR CONTROLS OVER EXPORTS

In recent decades there has been a tendency for governments to intervene in both sides of foreign trade activity, import and export, and an increasing number of government-to-government commitments. Controls over exports are exercised: (1) as a means of raising prices received on sales abroad; (2) in order to stimulate exports in a more advanced stage of production; (3) to regulate exports of products as they come into short supply as a means of preventing domestic prices from rising too much; and (4) for national and international security reasons.

Export taxes. The subject of export duties, as far as the United States is concerned, is dealt with specifically in two articles of the Constitution. Article I, Section IX, Paragraph 5 reads: "No tax or duty shall be laid on articles exported from any state." Article I, Section X, Paragraph 2, reads:

> No state shall, without the consent of the Congress, lay any impost or duties on imports or exports, except what may be absolutely necessary for executing its inspection laws; and the net produce of all duties and imposts, laid by any state on imports or exports, shall be for the use of the Treasury of the United States; and all such laws shall be subject to the revision and control of the Congress.

Hence, since Congress alone has the authority to levy such (export) duties, and since the Constitution prohibits a tax or duty on articles exported from any state, the policy to be followed by the United States is clear. The nature of control or regulation of exports by the United States is other than fiscal; it is qualitative and quantitative for revenue purposes. In fact, export taxes on primary commodities represent a principal source of government revenue in many developing countries.

Export taxes are also used for other objectives—for price stabilization or to furnish funds for specific industry undertakings. Moreover, they may be used selectively to influence the pattern of production in a way similar to government price supports. In 1960, for example, Sarawak removed its export duty on coconut oil, while that on copra was retained in order to stimulate the processing of copra. Or export taxes may be used in special circumstances, such as in India in 1966, following devaluation of the rupee.

At that time export taxes were imposed on a broad range of commodities in order to capture for the Government some of the gains accruing from larger exports stimulated by the devaluation.

Qualitative controls. In the United States qualitative requirements are imposed by the Grain Standards Act, which provides that grain cannot be exported (or shipped in domestic commerce) unless inspected and classified by an agent of the Department of Agriculture. Certification is also required for the export of apples, pears, and emperor grapes; certification in this case deals with grade, package marking, and quality. It is intended to prevent poorer qualities from misrepresenting established qualities or classifications. Certain other countries also require certification of exports to assure quality.

Quantitative controls. By far the more widespread controls are quantitative, applied for such purposes as security, health, sanitation, or conservation. Quantitative controls are also made effective by international agreement pertaining to the export trade in given products. Postwar activities of this type arose from the International Materials Conference and the Coordinating Committee on Export Controls (COCOM). More recently, formal intergovernmental commodity agreements gave rise to the use of quantitative export controls. Among products affected are tin, coffee, sugar, and cotton textiles.

One may be surprised at the extent to which quantitative controls are practiced by the United States, especially in view of pressures to expand exports in the 1960's as a means of overcoming balance of payments deficits. Overall, it may be stated that all export transactions with certain designated areas are subject to license; and all transactions in designated products, regardless of destination, are subject to license by the Department of Commerce unless the licensing function is the specific responsibility of another Government agency.

The most far-reaching of U.S. export controls are those that arise from the Export Control Act of 1949, as extended and amended by Public Law 89–63, 89th Congress. The act authorizes controls over exports for three purposes: national security, foreign policy, and short supply.

With two exceptions, commercial exports from the United States and its territories or possessions are prohibited unless the Department of Commerce has either issued a "validated license" or established a "general license" permitting such shipments. These two exceptions are exports from the continental United States to its territories and possessions and most exports to Canada for internal consumption.

A *validated license* is a formal license issued to an exporter by the Department of Commerce. A *general license* is a broad authorization issued by the Department of Commerce permitting certain exportations under specified conditions. Formal application and formal license are not needed for the latter; the authority to export is given in the Comprehensive Export Schedule, which specifies the conditions under which each general license may be used. The Comprehensive Export Schedule also contains regulations concerning the export of technical data, this also being subject to export control.

For operational and procedural purposes, the Department of Commerce maintains on a current basis the Commodity Control List,[4] a numerical listing by Schedule B, Revised, number,[5] of all commodities for which export licensing authority is exercised by the Department of Commerce. It identifies for each listed commodity the destinations for which a validated export license is required.

There are three major categories of country controls reflected in the Commodity Control List:

1. Commodities which require a validated license for exportation to all countries of the world (except for internal consumption in Canada). As of early 1965, there were 1,100 such listings.
2. Commodities which require a validated license for exportation to all countries *outside the Western Hemisphere but including Cuba* (there were 82 listings in this category).
3. Commodities which require a validated license for exportation only to Cuba, the Sino-Soviet bloc, and, in some instances, Hong Kong, Macao, Poland, and Rumania.

International coordination of export controls. Export control, which in the United States began in 1940, was continued after the war as a security measure, and was strengthened by passage of the Export Control Act of 1949. The security nature of postwar controls is best illustrated by the fact that the U.S. controls were integrated into an allied export control system, with export control on strategic goods imposed by several, if not all, of the allied powers. Some degree of uniformity of control was achieved through a Coordinating Committee on Export Controls (COCOM).[6] The list of items under common coordinated control has been rather constantly reduced, as world tensions abated. A major revision of the list took place in 1954, and

[4] The Commodity Control List superseded, effective January 1, 1965, the Positive List.

[5] The U.S. statistical system for exports.

[6] Members as of 1966 were the United Kingdom, France, Italy, the Netherlands, Belgium, Luxembourg, the United States, Norway, Denmark, Canada, the Federal Republic of Germany, Portugal, Greece, Turkey, and Japan.

there have been periodic list reviews since that time as a result of differing evaluations as to strategic importance of this or that item, pressures on companies to satisfy Bloc demands and thereby to create more jobs through production, and especially local pressures on companies not to lose sizable orders (and jobs, taxes, and profits) because of controls more restrictive than some would like to see. The U.S. export control system is substantially more restrictive than are those of our allies,[7] and in the late 1950's and mid-1960's frequent pressures developed to open up trading opportunities, especially to take advantage of and even to encourage more independent attitudes on the part of some of the eastern European satellite countries. In fact, President Johnson in early 1965 established a special committee recruited from business, education, and labor to explore all aspects of expanding such trade. That committee's report (sometimes referred to as the Miller Committee, after its chairman) was published in April 1965. Other reports, notably one by the Committee for Economic Development, also concluded that increased trade in nonstrategic goods is desirable. Part of this picture is also the flexibility available to the President in the determination of which countries are to enjoy most-favored-nation treatment in our tariff rates.

[7] The Commodity Control List is considerably longer than the Battle Act List, which relates to United States participation in COCOM.

Chapter VIII

Restrictive Business Practices

The subject of restrictive business practices in international trade is difficult but very important to the international businessman, the lawyer, and the economist.[1] It goes to the heart of the theory of freer trade and competition, out of which a greater international division of labor is permitted with goods produced able to be offered in wider markets, and under which market forces are freed and expected to yield the maximum of gross national production consistent therewith. Restrictive business practices, a term commonly applied to *private* practices or arrangements that restrain competition, limit access to markets, or encourage monopolistic control, take diverse forms ranging from informal gentlemen's agreements to formal and powerfully organized cartels. They are considered undesirable because they may limit the right to enter into business at all, in some cases, or they may limit the right to compete in a dynamic sense, even though one is not impeded from engaging in an otherwise legal undertaking.

When a government espouses the competitive, free-enterprise philosophy in its economic system, it cannot afford to have the expected objectives and benefits frustrated by restrictive private arrangements. Therefore, certain

[1] This chapter is not offered as legal guidance. Rather, it is a layman's understanding of some of the highlights of a specialized and complex part of the field of international business. The need for good counsel in given specific situations is obvious.

legislation and institutions pertaining to restrictive business practices have come into being. The subject of restrictive business practices covers a mélange of theory, law, regulation, and court tests; the latter are continuing with varying intensity, depending on the clarity of the law or regulation, on the zealousness of the government agencies charged with surveillance and enforcement, and on the similarity of a given set of circumstances to earlier ones, concerning which court decisions are taken as a guide to proper and safe action.

BASIC LEGISLATION

Several basic U.S. statutes and decisions apply to foreign trade, even though not specifically designed to meet a foreign business problem; others are more or less specifically tailored to serve a purpose in the regulation of international business.

Section 1 of the Sherman Act (1890) declares illegal every contract, combination in the form of trust or otherwise, or conspiracy in restraint of trade or commerce among the several states, or with foreign nations. Section 2 of the act makes it a crime to monopolize, or combine or conspire with any other person or persons to monopolize, any part of the trade or commerce among the several states, or with foreign nations.

Part of the Wilson Tariff Act (1894) makes illegal every combination, conspiracy, trust, agreement, or contract between two or more persons or corporations, either of which is an importer, that is intended to function ". . . in restraint of lawful trade, or of free competition in lawful trade or commerce, or to increase the market price in any part of the United States, of any imported article, or of any manufacture into which such imported article enters or is intended to enter." Under this law it would appear that price fixing in foreign trade, if it substantially affects prices in the United States, is unreasonable, and that the restriction of imports into the United States by agreement is similarly condemned.

The "rule of reason" (1898 and 1911) in application of the Sherman Act was enunciated in court decisions involving the Addyston Pipe and Steel Company, the Standard Oil Company of New Jersey, and the American Tobacco Company. Under this interpretation only unreasonable and undue restraints are meant to be included in the law. However, certain types of agreements are unreasonable, *per se,* and have been ruled to be so by court decisions. Among these are division of market territories and agreements to fix prices.[2] The amount of commerce that must be affected in order to be violative of laws in *per se* violations is not of consequence; the practices are condemned by their inherent nature or effect. Wilbur L. Fugate observes what he considers to be a basic error in comprehending the application of the rule of reason to foreign commerce. He points out that there must be the requisite effect on foreign commerce before there is jurisdiction under the Sherman Act. Only after this is established can the question arise as to whether the acts or contracts unreasonably restrain trade.[3]

The Clayton Act (1914), after defining "commerce" as including trade or commerce among the several states and with foreign nations, prohibits certain practices in connection therewith. Of obvious applicability to imports is the condemnation of price discrimination in the sale of goods within the United States. The act also makes it unlawful to sell or lease goods for use or resale in the United States on condition that the buyer or lessee will not deal in the goods of a competitor.

The Shipping Act of 1916 legalized shipping conferences by according them immunity from the application of antitrust laws of the United States on condition that they subject themselves to supervision and regulation by the Federal Maritime Board. The law requires common carriers by water, and engaged in foreign commerce, to file with the board every agreement which fixes or regulates transportation rates or fares.

The Webb-Pomerene Act (1918) makes an exception to the Sherman Act with respect to an association entered into by firms for the sole purpose of engaging in export trade and *actually engaging in such export trade* and as to acts done or contracts made by such association in the course of such export trade, if not in restraint of trade within the United States and not in restraint of the export trade of any domestic competitor of such association; provided also that the association does not do anything to artificially or intentionally enchance or depress prices of the same class of goods in the United States, or to substantially lessen or otherwise restrain trade in the United States.

The act contains the provision that the prohibition against ". . . unfair methods of competition in the Federal Trade Commission Act shall be construed as extending to unfair methods of competition used in export trade

[2] In the Socony Vacuum case the Supreme Court ruled that ". . . any combination formed for the purpose and with the effect of raising, depressing, fixing, pegging, or stabilizing the price of a commodity in interstate or foreign commerce is illegal, *per se*."

[3] Wilbur L. Fugate, *Foreign Commerce and the Antitrust Laws,* Little Brown and Company, Boston, 1958, p. 126.

against competitors engaged in export trade, even though the acts constituting such unfair methods are done without the territorial jurisdiction of the United States." Surveillance of the act is under the Federal Trade Commission, with which Webb-Pomerene association's must register and file annual reports.

As evolved, a Webb-Pomerene association may act as export sales agent for its members, promote conferences and agreements in export trade, exploit its members' products abroad, agree upon prices, terms, and sales policies in export trade, allocate export business among its members, arrange for insurance, freight rates, and cargo space, and collect and disseminate trade information concerning foreign markets.[4] Webb-Pomerene associations have never been important in U.S. export trade. Since 1918 a total of 230 associations have been formed, representing some 4,000 member exporters. Many of these did not last long, and the number existing in mid-1968 was 31. Nor have they been significant in overall trade; the value of exports attributable to them in recent years is in the neighborhood of 4 to 5 percent of the U.S. total.

The future of Webb-Pomerene associations may be less promising than it was for many years, if indeed they have a future, since in June 1967 the Department of Justice recommended repeal of the law. Among the points brought out by Assistant Attorney General Turner in his testimony before the Senate Antitrust Subcommittee were:

1. Even though the law applies to foreign commerce, it inevitably affects American consumers; the fixing of export prices may carry over to the domestic market.
2. It provides a precedent for foreign nations and makes it impossible to argue that they should limit the use of export cartels when our law allows their existence.

The Civil Aeronautics Act (1938) incorporates the same general provision as the Shipping Act of 1916 and makes it applicable to airlines. The Civil Aeronautics Board was established by this act as the board of control.

It should be evident from this brief identification of the major relevant laws that their existence and enforcement pose a number of practical, operational problems for the international businessman. Surely no one condones barefaced violation of laws of any type. But in the application of antitrust

[4] Walter S. Surrey and Crawford Shaw, *A Lawyer's Guide to International Business Transactions,* Joint Committee on Continuing Legal Education, Philadelphia, 1963, p. 636.

laws, in particular to foreign trade, it seems that there is ground for misunderstanding or at least for honest differences of opinion.

JURISDICTIONAL PROBLEMS

There is a question as to the extent to which American antitrust legislation can or should reach overseas. As an example, the American Chamber of Commerce in London took the view in 1955 that: "Our national interest requires that we stop applying our antitrust laws to activities outside the territorial limits of the United States."[5] Thus there is basically a question of, or perhaps a misunderstanding as to, jurisdiction. Many experts in the field share the view expressed by S. Powell Bridges:

> Wherever U.S. citizens or U.S. corporations are, or may go, U.S. courts have jurisdiction, and thus power, over them, though they deal through foreign corporations or operate through the medium of foreign agents. Where aliens, or alien corporations owned by aliens, or even instruments of foreign governments, restrain our trade, our law will reach them whenever they or their property enter the United States, its territories or possessions.[6]

A similar professional view is: "Our courts have assumed jurisdiction under the antitrust laws over acts and contracts substantially and directly affecting, or interfering with, U.S. foreign trade even though such acts were done, or contracts executed, outside of our borders."[7]

The conclusion, therefore, is that U.S. antitrust laws are not by design extraterritorial in application but pertain only to activities, no matter where performed, which substantially and directly affect or interfere with U.S. foreign trade. It appears that it is the effect within the United States or upon U.S. foreign commerce which is the test rather than where the contract is made or where it is to be performed.[8]

In the enforcement of action, it frequently turns out that documents or records are subpoenaed. Some international businesses have made it a point to keep sensitive records abroad, out of U.S. territory, in order to frustrate

[5] *The American Antitrust Laws and American Business Abroad,* American Chamber of Commerce in London, Inc., London, 1955, p. 29.

[6] S. Powell Bridges, "Antitrust Aspects of Doing Business Abroad," *Business Abroad and Export Trade,* September 21, 1964, p. 24.

[7] Fugate, *op. cit.,* p. 20.

[8] *Ibid.,* p. 40.

the Government's investigatory and enforcement proceedings. In a prominent case involving this point, the International Paper Company argued that some of its records were in Canada and that the board of directors (all residents of Canada) of its wholly owned Canadian subsidiary had passed a resolution forbidding removal of the records from Canada. Yet the court ruled, "That part of a corporation's records and documents are physically located beyond the confines of the United States does not excuse it from producing them if they are in its possession and the court has jurisdiction of the corporation. The test is control—not location—of the records."[9]

One of the more interesting tests along this line occurred in 1964 when the Maritime Administration attempted to obtain steamship conference documents (or information contained therein) from foreign lines that were members of conferences serving certain U.S. ports. This was in connection with the Government's investigation into the extent and effect of discriminatory ocean freight rates, and some of the foreign operators and conferences refused to make the information available to the Maritime Administration. The issue was settled by the foreign governments' agreeing, after about a year's negotiations, to accede to part of the U.S. Government's requests by providing the information as a bloc, for each conference, and not on the basis of individual country or company records.[10] The information was turned over to the Organization for Economic Cooperation and Development for circulation to all of the 15 governments concerned.

APPLICATION OF U.S. LAWS TO SPECIFIC SITUATIONS

The specific situations that may arise, and concerning which there may be serious and honest question as to the legality of certain practices related thereto, are so numerous as to be impossible to catalog. However, the following selected situations are common to many, if not most, international business operations. Reference to them will at least suggest the need for caution and for obtaining expert legal counsel.

Appointment of exclusive distributor abroad. It is usual for an American manufacturer or exporter to appoint exclusive agents or distributors abroad. In fact, the foreign businessman wishes just such an appointment for his own protection. He invests time and money in setting up a business, and he also forgoes alternative opportunities. Such an arrangement has been found not to be illegal, *per se,* in a number of rulings. However, there is

[9] *Ibid.,* p. 80.

[10] Hearings before Subcommittee on Federal Procurement and Regulation, Joint Economic Committee, 89th Congress, 1st Session, Part 2, May 27, 1965, p. 402.

danger in appointing a *competitor* in a foreign country as exclusive agent, particularly if the competitor appoints the American company as its exclusive distributor in the United States. Such an arrangement may be considered an agreement not to compete.[11]

Restrictions on distributors' handling of products of others. The danger here is the possible closing of substantial foreign outlets to other American exporters. Therefore, one would be advised to look cautiously before entering an agreement that obligates a foreign distributor to purchase all of his *American* requirements (of the same or a competing product) from one exporter. Obviously, U.S. laws would have no effect on restricting a distributor from handling the products of competitors from countries other than the United States. There could also, of course, be no complaint against a foreign independent businessman's voluntary decision to confine his purchases to one American exporter. Moreover, such considerations would have to involve the possibility of "substantial" effect on the commerce of the United States before they could be adjudged to be an unreasonable restraint of trade.

Territorial restrictions on distributors. The moment a foreign distributor is given an "exclusive" for a certain country or territory, it means that the manufacturer or exporter agrees that no one else will be given distribution rights (except those which may be reserved) for the same product in the same territory. This is a plus in justifying the distributor's investment of money, time, and reputation in creating and maintaining a distribution system for the American exporter's product. It is also a plus for the exporter who, by doing so, is in a better position to expect, and even demand, the full cooperation of the distributor who, presumably, should not then dilute his interest and effort.

But suppose someone given exclusive rights in a country or territory should decide to spill over into the territory which is the exclusive domain of another, similarly decreed by the American exporter. What can an exporter do to protect the assigned markets from predatory action by others who also have assigned markets? If a distributor has been commissioned to sell in France, but then turns around and sells in Spain as well, it may be fairly concluded that he is exceeding his authority, whether Spain has or has not been given as an "exclusive" to anyone else. It may be that the American exporter is in the process of negotiating such an exclusive in Spain, the attraction of which would be tarnished by such activity on the part of the French distributor.

[11] The most thorough discussion of this subject appears to be in Fugate, *op. cit.*, pp. 114–123. See also, Bridges, *op. cit.*, p. 22.

The exporter has grounds for stating that the French distributor has violated his agreement. And if the contract includes a punitive or corrective clause to which such action can be related—even to the point of termination of the contract if the exporter finds this to be in his best overall interest—a mechanism will have been provided for effective protection. Another way in which such an "exclusive" can be protected is by providing that the exclusive distributor will be entitled to a commission on sales made by others in his territory. The problem here is to prove how much was sold to and by whom.

Price-fixing arrangements with exclusive distributors. There are two areas of major interest here—one relating to imports, which are sold in the U.S. market, and one relating to exports, which are sold abroad. Insofar as resale price maintenance within the United States is concerned, the Miller-Tydings Act (1937) makes an exception to the Sherman Act with respect to minimum resale price fixing by a producer or distributor of his trademarked goods, under specified conditions, when such agreements are lawful in the state of resale.[12] In the case of American exports, Fugate states that there is very little law regarding the American producer who fixes the resale price of goods sold abroad.[13]

RESTRICTIVE BUSINESS PRACTICES ABROAD

There are two areas of fundamental disharmony, actual or potential, between restrictive business attitudes and tolerances in the United States and abroad. One is the question of which national laws apply to specific business affairs—the question of jurisdiction; the other is, within such laws, what can or cannot be done by an international businessman. This poses a constant problem for the international businessman, not only because there is no international law, as such, to guide private business practice, but the existing statutes are couched in broad terms that do not relate to specific practices. Therefore, court decisions are very important; but these are sometimes reversed, and the situations faced may not be identical to those on which earlier decisions were rendered.

Perhaps the historical uncertainty may best be illustrated by the differences in the antitrust philosophy and legislation of the United States, at one extreme, and by the long-time and deep-rooted acceptance of cartels in Europe and in Japan (the Zaibatsu institution).

[12] Fugate, *op. cit.*, p. 105.
[13] *Ibid.*, p. 106.

PROGRESS TOWARD INTERNATIONAL HARMONIZATION

While there is no international framework of common rules, some progress in this direction has been achieved, expecially in the postwar period. Some private practices that are now widely considered to be restrictive have come under critical scrutiny because of their potential for frustrating the benefits of postwar liberal trade policies and economic integration. As identified by the GATT secretariat in 1959,[14] such policies are those which aim to:

- Influence prices or conditions of sale, purchase, or lease.
- Restrict output, production capacity, and production lines.
- Allocate markets.
- Set up joint sales or purchasing services or pool profits.
- Hinder the development or the exploitation of technical processes, or unduly extend the use of rights arising out of patents, trademarks, and the like.
- Eliminate outside competition.

One of the most important postwar changes in attitudes toward international business practices has been that pertaining to the rules of competition. There has been widespread acceptance by Free World countries in the postwar period of the undesirability of restrictive business practices. Consequently, many countries passed legislation subscribing to the principles of free enterprise in an attempt to secure the maximum amount of competition thought to be practicable and consistent with other national objectives. Of course, there were differences in detail and, in some cases, even in principle, but on the whole the countries managed to attain a high degree of similarity in the laws.

The following chronological listings of significant action, taken internationally and nationally in the postwar period and dealing with restrictive business practices, were developed by Lee Loevinger, then Assistant Attorney General in charge of the Antitrust Division, U.S. Department of Justice. They are taken from his address, "Antitrust Law in the Modern World," which was presented at a meeting of the New York State Bar Association in New York City on January 25, 1962.

[14] *Restrictive Business Practices,* General Agreement on Tariffs and Trade, Geneva, May 1959, p. 16.

International—GATT

1945 "Proposals for Expansion of World Trade and Employment," published by Department of State, followed by invitation to 15 other countries to join with the United States in preparing an international conference on trade and employment.

1946 First draft of charter for an International Trade Organization.

1947 First large-scale postwar international trade conference held in Geneva. Out of this came the General Agreement on Tariffs and Trade (GATT). The second part, containing general provisions relating to trade and competition, was expected to remain in force pending final approval of an International Trade Organization.

1948 Havana Conference, out of which came the document known as the Havana Charter for an International Trade Organization. Chapter V of this charter dealt with restrictive business practices.

1951 ECOSOC resolution recommended international cooperation in the restriction of business practices that restrain competition.

International—OECD

1948 Organization for European Economic Cooperation (OEEC) formed.

1953 European Productivity Agency set up by OEEC. It sponsored a group of experts on restrictive business practices, which met periodically from 1953 to 1961.

1960 OEEC replaced by Organization for Economic Cooperation and Development (OECD).

1961 U.S. adherence thereto ratified by Senate. Council of OECD officially established a Committee of Experts on Restrictive Business Practices.

National Legislative Activity

1947 Japan passed an Anti-Monopoly Act under the strong influence of the occupying American authorities. (Japan had been the first country to introduce legislation providing for compulsory cartelization).[15]

1948 Great Britain enacted a Monopolies and Restrictive Practices Act and later, in 1956, the Restrictive Trade Practices Act. Restrictive practices must be publicly registered and the Restrictive Practices Court decides whether the restrictions are contrary to public interest.

[15] *International Cartels,* a League of Nations Memorandum, Department of Economic Affairs, United Nations Publication Sales No.: 1948. II. D.2, United Nations, New York, p. 10.

1951 Austria enacted a cartel law (amended in 1958 and re-enacted in 1959) which required the registration of cartels that may restrict competition, and which prohibits cartel abuses.

1953 Norway, Sweden, and Ireland passed laws on the subject. The Norwegian law in general forbids restrictive arrangements by associations or groups to fix prices, profits, or terms of sale. Resale price fixing is subject to express approval of the Price Director. The Swedish law prohibits restraints of competition which unduly affect prices, limit production, or impede trade by others. The Irish act established a Fair Trade Commission to prohibit restrictive trade practices and formulate their trading rules.

1954 }
1958 } France issued new supplements to earlier law. In France several restrictive business practices are specifically forbidden, such as refusals to sell, tying agreements, and the fixing of resale prices or margins. Expressly prohibited also are concerted actions that can have the effect of interfering with competition by preventing the reduction of prices or by encouraging artificial increases in price.

1955 Denmark passed a Monopolies and Restrictive Trade Practices Act. It provides for registration of restrictive agreements and prohibits most restrictions upon resale prices.

1956 The Netherlands passed an Economic Competition Act, which is said to be perhaps the best example of what is called the "abuse principle" as contrasted with "prohibition principle." All restrictive agreements must be registered. The Minister of Economic Affairs may declare a restrictive agreement to be binding on all those in the trade.

1957 Germany and Finland passed significant legislation. As a matter of principle, the German law makes all cartel agreements and resolutions ineffective or invalid, subject to numerous exception. This change in attitude toward cartels was influenced by laws and ordinances imposed by the Allied Powers following World War II. Finland's Law for the Control of Restraints of Competition in Trade requires all restrictive agreements to be reported to a cartel authority. Arrangements involving concerted action may be undertaken only by special permission of the authority.

1960 Belgium and Canada passed new legislation on the subject. Belgium enacted a Law on the Protection Against the Abuse of Economic Power. Specific or detailed prohibitions apparently are not identified, but an elaborate procedure exists for investigating and terminating abuses. Canada, which has had an antitrust statute since 1889, amended its law in 1960. Prosecution of restrictive business practices is by criminal, not civil, proceedings. It is an offense to arrange with another person to take or refrain from taking certain actions, such as undue limitation of trade or of production, price fixing, or restriction of competition.

INFLUENCE OF INTEGRATION MOVES

Another strong influence in the two-decade evolution toward reduction or control of private restrictive business practices was the movement toward economic integration. It appears to have been here that focus was most sharpened on the conflict between government efforts to open up international markets and private arrangements in conflict therewith.

The earliest large-scale movement was the European Coal and Steel Community (ECSC), the treaty for which was signed in 1951. The treaty contained the following provisions:

> All agreements among enterprises, all decisions of associations of enterprises, and all concerted practices tending, directly or indirectly, to prevent, restrict or distort the normal operation of competition within the common market are hereby forbidden, and in particular those tending to: fix or determine prices; restrict or control production, technical development, or investments; allocate markets, products, customers, or sources of supply.

ECSC was followed in 1957 by the European Economic Community (Rome Treaty) and by the European Free Trade Association (Stockholm Treaty), both of which addressed themselves to the rules of competition. Competition is endorsed in categorical terms by the EEC as one of several measures to achieve aims of the treaty. The main provisions pertaining to the subject are in Part Three of the treaty, particularly Articles 85–90, which deal with restrictive business practices. Article 85 reads in part:

> 1. The following are incompatible with the Common Market and are prohibited: all agreements between enterprises, all decisions by associations or enterprises, and all concerted practices which are likely to affect adversely trade between the Member States, and which have the object or effect of preventing, restricting, or distorting competition within the Common Market, in particular those which:
>
> (a) Directly or indirectly fix buying or selling prices or other trading terms.

(b) Effect the sharing of markets or sources of supply.
(c) Apply to trade partners unequal conditions in respect of equivalent transactions, thereby placing them at a competitive disadvantage.
(d) Make the conclusion of a contract subject to the acceptance by trade partners of additional goods or services which are not by their nature or by the custom of the trade related to the subject matter of such a contract.

2. The agreements or decisions prohibited by this Article are null and void. . . .

One can see from the foregoing that it is not a question of evaluating whether a cartel is good or bad only in its effect. It is more than a question of controlling restrictive practices *only if their end result is undesirable*—or if they abuse their position.

The roots from which agreement on this point had to be hammered out are indicated by discussions leading up to the EEC Commission's Regulation on Restrictive Practices; they illustrate the split of opinion within the Community. For example, it was argued that the principle of misuse had been traditional in previous proposals for international supervision of cartels. Another view was that competition is not an end in itself; the objective to be sought is not a predetermined market structure, but economic progress.[16] Still another view was that the EEC treaty's provisions for restrictive practices could only be accomplished within the framework of common economic policy, which then did not exist.[17]

On the other hand there was the concept that: "Competition is and should be the regulating principle of the Common Market, since economic progress and a competitive system are practically synonymous."[18]

In implementing Articles 85 and 86 of the Rome Treaty, it was proposed that the regulation would reach existing agreements as well as those entered into after it came into effect. This was because of the need for imposing a uniform control over restrictive business practices that had evolved in varying national degrees over the decades and under different national laws. The issue was put on the track by requiring that all companies in the Common Market had to notify the EEC Commission of the existence of the following types of agreements, without which notification the agreements would be considered unenforceable:

[16] *Cartel Policy and the Common Market,* Political and Economic Planning, London, 1962, p. 207.

[17] *Ibid.*

[18] *Ibid.,* p. 208.

- The direct or indirect fixing of minimum, maximum, or fixed prices for merchandise or services.
- The limitation of production, market, or investment.
- Market sharing by regions, by customers, or by other criteria.
- Agreements preventing, restraining, or regulating importation or exportation between member states.

Notification was not required of agreements between only two companies which had the following for their sole purpose:

- Resale price restrictions agreement between a seller and a buyer.
- Limitations in the exercise of rights imposed on the user under patents or trademarks.
- Exclusive rights to purchase or sell between buyer and seller.
- Exclusive representation for specified products or services of an enterprise.

Just as national attitudes toward restrictive business practices are not uniform, neither are the attitudes of all common markets or free trade areas. For example, the European Free Trade Association (EFTA) regards restrictive practices as incompatible with the convention only insofar as they frustrate the benefits expected from the removal or absence of duties and quantitative restrictions on trade among member states. Article 15 of the Stockholm Convention declares incompatible with the convention certain practices whose effect is as just indicated. In general, it would appear that the EEC regulations are more rigid and general in application, while those of the EFTA are a bit more tolerant, looking to the element of abuse as the matter to be controlled.

Chapter IX

Taxation of International Business

The taxation of business carried on internationally is so complex and specialized a problem that generalizing does not provide an answer or even a dependable guide. The skeletal survey given in this chapter, however, will obviously suggest that resolution of any problem in this area depends on the combination of factors to be considered in each case; the need for competent legal counsel as a practical necessity will be evident. Most of the references herein pertain to income taxes, since they are normally the heaviest in burden. They are of special interest because of treatment of income tax credit in the United States and because they are the subject of major efforts by governments to avoid double taxation. The variety of taxes, both direct and indirect, however, merits the full consideration of all types applicable in a given situation.

While every business is subject to tax on international operations, the fuller international dimensions of taxation have primary interest to and impact on those companies that operate in more than one country. Some 900 leading U.S. companies, with foreign investments of over $2 million each, are in this category.

Taxes are part of the cost of goods sold internationally. Their cost cannot normally be shifted by higher prices to the purchaser when competition is not subject to an equivalent tax burden. But to the extent that taxes can be reduced by good management, internationally competitive costs are thereby reduced. Companies cannot afford, competitively, to have their incomes disappear unnecessarily into the hands of tax collectors; the officers responsible would not long hold their jobs if they did. As stated by a leading expert in the field, "To overlook tax costs in any foreign operation today is to lose, possibly for all time, a portion of the ultimate earnings of your company for it and for your stockholders."[1]

What makes the final impact of taxation interesting and important to international business is that many countries grant relatively attractive tax treatment to companies organized under their laws or operating in them through a "permanent establishment." The alert and responsible officer should at least consider whether there is advantage to his company in availing itself of this possible privilege. What is suggested is that businessmen must apply *tax planning* to their international operations to avoid paying unnecessary taxes, even after government treaties looking toward the avoidance of double taxation. Moreover, in tax planning, taxes other than those based on income play an important role. For example, customs duties are especially significant in view of widespread preferential trading arrangements.

TAX JURISDICTION

International law does not specify who has the right to tax, nor does it limit the scope of any country's tax jurisdiction. A country can tax what it wishes (but to be practical, it must be able to enforce collection), and there appears to be no recorded case of a national court condemning double taxation as violating international law.[2]

In the academic discipline of political economy, there is no clear theory of tax jurisdiction. Laws differ, based on economic and political necessity. The taxation of income earned from international business activities, however, gives rise to the essentially economic problem of reconciling varying tax claims of overlapping national tax jurisdiction. Today, in practice, policies with respect to foreign-source income vary according to the nature of income or of the asset to be taxed, the nationality or residence of the taxpayer, and the time or point at which the income becomes taxable.

The two *major* differences in the tax systems employed by different countries appear to rest on the residence of the firm or individual (which would determine whether it or he is subject to taxing jurisdiction) and the

[1] Walter A. Slowinski, "United States Taxation of Foreign Source Income," *Taxes and International Business,* National Association of Manufacturers, New York, 1965, p. 7.

[2] *Ibid.*

source of income. As to firms, it is common practice for the taxpayer's country of residence to tax on all income earned within the country as well as on foreign-earned income when, generally, earnings are remitted from abroad, but on an imputed basis in some cases, even though not remitted. Then credit for income (or income type of) taxes paid foreign governments is allowed against the tax due. On the other hand, if credit is not allowed against the tax due, certain taxes paid abroad may be incorporated as a charge against income. In some cases, a credit for taxes may be allowed even though the taxes were waived (in order to attract the investment) by, say, a less-developed country in which the earnings were sourced. In addition, some countries, such as the Netherlands, Belgium, and France, or political subdivisions of a country (as in the case of Switzerland) may exempt foreign earnings from income tax or tax them at a reduced rate, under certain specified or negotiated conditions.

Policy of the United States. The United States, on the other hand, applies its own corporate tax to the earnings of foreign branches of American firms and, in some cases, to a subsidiary's profits, even though no dividends are declared. The Internal Revenue Act of 1962 substantially modified the former arrangement of taxing by U.S. authorities only when income earned abroad came effectively into possession of the U.S. shareholder. This point is discussed later in this chapter.

U.S. jurisdiction for taxing foreign-business income is prescribed by Congress in our internal revenue laws, which impose a tax for each taxable year on the taxable income of every corporation. No mention is made as to the chartering authority. With the adoption of the Federal income tax in 1913, the United States imposed its personal and corporate income taxes both on income arising within its boundaries, regardless of the nationality or residence of the earner thereof, and on foreign-source income of resident individuals and of corporations chartered within the United States, initially with foreign taxes deductible from taxable income. This latter feature was amended in 1918 when income taxes paid abroad were made deductible from income taxes due to the U.S. Government. Thus the right to tax both by domicile of the income recipient and by source of income was asserted from the beginning of our employment of a tax based on income.

Some countries ignore the place of incorporation as a basis for income tax jurisdiction. Rather, the emphasis is on location and control of the place of corporate management. This is the case for the United Kingdom, Canada, Australia, and New Zealand. Corporations so subject to designation as residents are then taxable on their income from all sources, generally with credit for taxes paid abroad.

While persons subject to U.S. income tax may appear to be subject to tax on all of their income from whatever source derived, numeorus exceptions and refinements in application have evolved in order to arrive equitably at taxable income. Some examples are:

- Foreign corporations engaged in business in the United States are taxable only on income received from U.S. sources and, when so provided by tax treaty, only if they operate through a "permanent establishment."
- Nonresident aliens and foreign corporations not engaged in business in the United States but receiving income from within the United States in the form of dividends, interest, rents, and royalties are taxable only at the rate of 30 percent. This rate may be lower if the income recipients are persons of a foreign country with which a tax convention providing therefor has been negotiated.
- Corporations chartered in the United States are allowed to credit against their income tax liability to the U.S. Government the amount of income tax, or tax in lieu of income tax, paid by them to the foreign country in which the income is sourced. In addition, certain exclusions may apply, such as for companies engaged primarily in earning income in U.S. possessions; and in the case of Western Hemisphere Trade Corporations, there are deductions in the rates of tax applicable.

Direct and derivative credit. Until 1918, as mentioned earlier, the foreign income taxes paid were allowed as deductions from *income* taxable in the United States. The sharp rise in income tax rates during the war period, however, led to the adoption in 1918 of the foreign tax credit concept, under which income taxes paid abroad may be credited against taxes due the United States. This was intended to ease the restrictive effects of heavy multiple taxation on business operations abroad. The United States was the first country to apply the foreign tax credit on a worldwide basis as a means of relieving the burdens of double taxation.[3]

Credit for income taxes paid abroad is of two types, direct and derivative. An example of the *direct* case would be the imposition of a tax by another country on the *branch* of a U.S. corporation, levied against income arising within its borders. The levy is directly against the United States corporation. The possibility of *derivative* credit, on the other hand, arises when

[3] Peggy Brewer Richman, *Taxation of Foreign Investment Income,* Johns Hopkins Press, Baltimore, 1963, p. 47.

the tax is imposed on the foreign *subsidiary* or *subsubsidiary* of the U.S. parent. Provision is made, depending on the situation, for the U.S. parent to utilize the credit when it receives a dividend from its subsidiary or when it is taxed by the United States on profits earned abroad but not distributed as dividends. The derivative credit can be used by a U.S. corporation if it owns 10 percent or more of the voting stock of its foreign subsidiary; it is also available for taxes imposed against subsubsidiaries if the subsidiary in which the U.S. parent has at least 10 percent participation owns 50 percent or more of the subsubsidiary. Insofar as availability of this derivative tax credit is concerned, the 1962 Internal Revenue Act provided for a differentiation in the treatment of income taxes paid abroad, depending on whether the subsidiary or subsubsidiary is in a developed or less-developed country.

There was, as may have been expected, heated opposition to several features of the Internal Revenue Act of 1962. It was argued vehemently that a foreign corporation, even though owned by a U.S. enterprise, is a person of the foreign country chartering it, and therefore the United States should not have the right to tax the income it earns abroad until such income is brought back to the U.S. parent as dividends or capital gains. On the other hand, it was argued, the history of international claims settlement shows that the nationality of a subsidiary will be overlooked when the parent wants it to be. For example, it was reasoned that U.S. parents expect the U.S. Government to protect their foreign interests in whatever form they may be (even for a foreign subsidiary corporation) in case of confiscation or expropriation by a foreign government. Hence the basic question was whether the corporation, as a legal entity, or the corporate enterprise is the business unit subject to tax. The decision was in favor of the latter.

THE TAX BASE

A company doing business abroad is subject to a variety of taxes resting on different bases. Some of these taxes are paid by all companies, whether operating profitably or not. Typical of this type is the property tax, based on the assessed value of real estate. Other examples are payroll taxes, based on a company's wages and salaries (these taxes are quite high in certain countries) ; a capital tax, based on invested capital; stamp and registration taxes, such as on transfers of stock certificates or real estate; and taxes on the registration of leases or license agreements.

The big problem is not with the foregoing but with taxes based on income and/or on the distribution of such income, since the rates differ widely and, in some cases, are exceptionally heavy. Earnings may be derived from several sources, and the definition of what income is, for tax purposes, and the specification of which expenses or credits are allowable against it represent an area of significant variance between taxing jurisdictions. For example, capital gains may not be considered as income subject to tax in some countries; in other countries, which do tax such gains as income, the tax may apply at the same rate as ordinary operating earnings. Or they may be taxed at a differential rate, as in the United States. Another factor which gives rise to differences in taxable income is the treatment of depreciation; the permissible rates differ among countries. Still another variable is investment allowances or credits; this may be an item to consider in new investments abroad, expecially in less-developed countries.

TAX RATES

Once the amount of taxable income (the tax base) has been determined, the next and probably most important feature is the rate of tax, which may be "ordinary"—applicable to all taxable income, or "excess"—applicable to such profits as exceed a given level. The ordinary rate of income tax varies widely among countries. For example, Surrey and Shaw[4] cite the following countries as having a low tax rate:

Country	*Percent*
Nicaragua	12
Paraguay	19
Ecuador	22
El Salvador	24
Honduras	25
Panama	26

Surrey and Shaw cite the following countries as having a high tax rate:

Country	*Percent*
India	58
Pakistan	64
Burma	69.4
Uruguay	75

[4] Walter S. Surrey and Crawford Shaw, *A Lawyer's Guide to International Business Transactions,* Joint Committee on Continuing Legal Education, Philadelphia, 1963, p. 206.

These rates would be applicable to income of a locally incorporated subsidiary of a U.S. corporation doing business in the countries named. There are, also, a few countries known as "tax havens," with exceptionally low tax rates and liberal interpretations of taxable income. Income "sourced" in them could, until 1962, avoid the U.S. tax and that of other relatively high taxing authorities by being retained in the low-rate country and by not being paid out as dividends to owners in the United States. The Internal Revenue Act of 1962, however, rendered tax-haven operations rather meaningless by declaring that income earned by *controlled* foreign subsidiaries of U.S. companies would in general be subject to the U.S. income tax, though not brought into the United States, by being declared as dividends to the American parent.

BASIC CONCEPTS AND DEFINITIONS

The Internal Revenue Act of 1962, and the wide and heated attention it received, brought into prominence some concepts and definitions that are and will be fundamental to the practitioner and student of international business. The alert businessman should be aware of them all for optimum international tax advantage.

Controlled foreign corporation. This designation was made in the Internal Revenue Act of 1962. It refers to a foreign corporation in which more than 50 percent of the voting stock is owned by U.S. shareholders, directly or indirectly, each of whom owns 10 percent or more of the stock of the corporation. Under the act, income (as earned, regardless of whether declared as dividends or not) of such foreign corporations is currently taxable to U.S. shareholders owning 10 percent or more of the stock, to the extent that the corporation has "Subpart F income" (income derived from insurance of U.S. risks, or foreign-base-company income) or invests earnings in U.S. property. This income is not to be taxed currently to U.S. shareholders, however; that is, it is not to be taxed before distribution in the form of dividends, if foreign-base-company income represents 30 percent or less of the gross income of the controlled foreign corporation. On the other hand, if foreign-base-company income exceeds 70 percent of the gross income of the controlled foreign corporation, its entire gross income is treated as foreign-base-company income and is therefore taxable when currently earned. The presumption is that control of the corporation, so narrowly held by dominant U.S. interests, confers to the U.S. interests the means to dictate choice of the income date and therefore of tax liability.

Foreign-base-company income. A foreign-base company is one established abroad and commonly used as a holding company to own and control corporate subsidiaries or branches in third countries, and to hold and license the use of industrial property rights. Its income, subject to special taxing provisions, is that which may be classified as *passive* in nature (dividends, interest, rents, royalties, and so forth), arising from investment rather than from the conduct of a business; or as *tax-haven* income, earned by foreign corporations from trade or business activities, with the activities involved having no economic or business connection with the foreign country of incorporation, and with the activities involving a shifting of income from a related party. In other words, income in this category must be derived by purchase from or sale to a related person, and the products or services involved must be sold for use outside the country in which the controlled company is organized. In either of these cases special taxing provisions hold, which render the income taxable currently whether declared as income to the parent or not. The regulations, however, exclude the following categories from foreign-base-company income:

1. Dividends, interest, and gains from qualified investments in less-developed countries.
2. Income derived from aircraft and ships.
3. Controlled foreign operations which do not have the effect of substantial reduction of income or similar taxes.

The regulations are complex and warrant detailed study for precision in given situations and for changes or modifications that will affect future specific cases.

Foreign-personal-holding-company income. Except as otherwise provided, U.S. shareholders who qualify are taxed on undistributed foreign-personal-holding-company income. A foreign-personal-holding-company is a foreign corporation more than 50 percent of whose stock is owned by five or fewer U.S. natural persons and at least 60 percent of whose income for the first taxable year (50 percent thereafter) is passive, that is, from rents, dividends, interest, royalties, gains from securities or commodities transactions, and similar nonbusiness activities. In order to avoid this tax bite, some people have formed foreign investment companies in which five or less U.S. persons do not own 50 percent of the stock; in that case, of course, they lose absolute control over its direction. In 1962, Congress reduced some of the attraction of foreign investment companies by requiring that gains from sales or exchanges of such stock are to be treated as ordinary income rather than as capital gain, to the extent of earnings and profits of the foreign investment company. This, in effect, makes such income taxable at a higher rate for most persons to whom a foreign investment company would be advantageous in the area of taxation.

Export trade corporation. This is a controlled foreign corporation which derives 90 percent or more of its gross income from outside the United States and 75 percent of its gross income from export trade. For this purpose, "export trade income" is defined as income from the sale by the controlled foreign corporation (not by the U.S. parent to unrelated persons) of goods produced in the United States. A company so qualifying may exclude a specified percentage of its gross receipts or of its promotional expenses, whichever is less, from its otherwise currently taxable foreign-base-company income. The company is required, further, to reinvest its excludable income in assets designed to promote further exports. Apparently, this inducement is not widely used. One authority notes that somewhat less than 2 percent of the companies involved in foreign operations were able to utilize the provisions just mentioned because of the limitations on deferral which are contained in the act.[5]

WESTERN HEMISPHERE TRADE CORPORATIONS

Reference was made earlier to exclusions, deductions, and credits as a factor in international business arrangements, and especially to their influence on the type of legal organization established to conduct such activities. One of the most important of such special arrangements—perhaps the most important as far as the United States is concerned—is the provision, begun in 1942, of a 14-point reduction in the U.S. tax due by a company that can qualify as a Western Hemisphere Trade Corporation. In view of U.S. corporate tax rates, this makes for a maximum rate of 15.6 percent on income not exceeding $35,300 and of 34 percent (instead of 48 percent) on income over that amount.[6]

To qualify for this benefit, the corporation, which must be chartered in the United States, must meet three specifications:

1. All business, except incidental purchases, must be done in the Western Hemisphere.

[5] Slowinski, *op. cit.,* p. 9.

[6] For a detailed discussion of Western Hemisphere Trade Corporations, see Michael A. Allara, "Court Rulings Seen Spurring Exporters' Interest in Western Hemisphere Trade Corporations," *International Commerce Magazine,* U.S. Department of Commerce, Washington, D.C., December 19, 1966, p. 5.

2. Ninety percent of its gross income must be from the active conduct of a trade or business. Determination of gross income for this purpose requires the exclusion of royalties from licensing and of dividends, interest, and gains from transactions in securities.
3. Ninety-five percent of its gross income must be derived from sources outside the United States.

Western Hemisphere Trade Corporations are rather widely used in connection with export operations. An important point to note in weighing the advantage of the arrangement is that, since the corporation must be chartered in the United States, its entire income is subject to tax as currently earned. On the other hand, U.S. taxes on income earned by a foreign affiliate may be deferred in some cases (for example, in a less-developed country) until such income is received by a U.S. shareholder.

ALLOCATION AND ADJUSTMENT OF INCOME BETWEEN RELATED ENTERPRISES

When a company is engaged in international business and its operations are subject to tax not only by the United States but also by foreign taxing authorities, the allocation of expenses and income between parent and subsidiary or branch is of practical interest not only to the business entity but to each government as well. The opportunity to make these allocations deliberate arises no matter what system for taxing foreign-earned income is adopted, and the basic problem is to avoid abuses, as far as government is concerned. If income can properly be "sourced" abroad, a U.S. company may, by operating through a foreign subsidiary, and with due allowance for the requirements of the Internal Revenue Act of 1962, defer its U.S. tax on certain of its income earned abroad until repatriated to the United States. The subsidiary represents a permanent establishment, however, and this subjects it to tax by the foreign country. Deferral enables more rapid accumulation of capital, but the capital must be held abroad. Restraints under the balance of payments emergency may preclude the holding of such assets abroad. In effect, part of such capital (that which would be paid in income tax if brought to the United States as a dividend) may be said to represent "interest free" funds so long as used abroad. Moreover, many foreign countries impose a tax on dividends to foreigners, so, by withholding dividends, this tax may also be deferred for a while. The abuse of disguised dividends, in the form of long-term loans by a foreign subsidiary to its parent in the United States, was checked by the 1962 act.

Though not a new concept in U.S. tax practice, the right of the Treasury to examine income allocation practices was strengthened in 1962. Under this section of the law, the Commissioner of Internal Revenue is empowered to adjust incomes within groups of commonly controlled corporations in order that true incomes will be more accurately reflected and that tax avoidance or evasion may be prevented. For example, he has authority to rule that goods sold by a U.S. exporter to its foreign subsidiary should have been taken into the income of the U.S. exporter at a higher price, and therefore the income subject to U.S. tax would be increased. The basic concept followed by the Treasury and incorporated into new proposed regulations in 1965 and 1966, concerning income allocation, is that for tax purposes such transactions must be at arm's length. At the same time the Treasury announced that the Internal Revenue Service would allocate income, for tax purposes, only in "significant" cases and not in instances where "minimal" amounts are involved.[7]

RELIEF FROM DOUBLE TAXATION

Any consideration of taxation in international business would omit an important aspect if it did not consider arrangements established by governments to exempt companies in international business from the obligation to pay some or all of the taxes that would be levied if the business were domestic only. The necessity for this arises because two taxing jurisdictions may claim the right to tax the same property or income.

Here we concern ourselves with the steps taken by governments, unilaterally and bilaterally (not yet multilaterally), to mitigate the impact of potentially dual taxes on international business. In recognition of the fact that jurisdiction is a matter of staking out one's claim, so to speak, governments have taken two steps which lead to modifying the burden of a company's being taxed on the same income in two jurisdictions. The first of these is unilateral and consists of provisions in the respective tax laws for credits, against income or against tax due, for taxes paid abroad. As mentioned earlier, this is common practice on the part of capital-exporting countries, and, in reality, it recognizes the primacy of claim to tax by the country in which the income is sourced. The second step taken by many countries

[7] U.S. Department of the Treasury press release, Washington, D.C., August 1, 1966.

is bilateral; a country agrees by treaty to share with another, on a prearranged basis, the taxes imposed on business conducted in the territory of one country by nationals of the other country.

Capital-exporting countries would appear to benefit from the device of tax treaties because their "residual" claims on the basis of residence or nationality are thereby better recognized; and the capital-importing countries would appear to benefit because their primary claim to taxing income at source is better recognized. Some benefit may also inure to the taxing authorities from administrative arrangements to aid each other in the collection of taxes by exchange of information; on this point, the companies and individuals concerned are rather thoroughly dissatisfied. There is also some advantage to the negotiation of a network of such treaties in that they tend to bring about more uniformity in tax treatment between countries. No multilateral treaties have been entered on the problem of double taxation but, as will be seen later, a draft convention has been drawn up by the OECD for possible adoption by countries when they negotiate bilaterally. There have been some proposals for negotiating multilateral tax treaties within the Central American Common Market and the Latin American Free Trade Association,[8] but as of mid-1968 nothing along this line had been accomplished.

Treaties for relief from double taxation are common and exist between many of the major countries of the world, especially capital-exporting countries, and between them and certain of the less-developed countries. Many European countries are signatories to ten or more conventions dealing with the subject, the country with the highest number (approximately 70) being the United Kingdom. On the other hand, and especially among the less-developed countries, some have only two or three, or even none, as in the case of Venezuela.

That the problem is general and is something of an impediment to wider economic relations was evidenced at least as far back as the early 1920's when the League of Nations convened a panel of experts to consider the theoretical aspects of the problem.[9] It issued a report in 1923 and suggested a policy of exempting income at the source and of full taxation of income in the country of residence of the recipient. Moreover, it dismissed the tax credit approach.[10] Later attention was given the problem by the United Nations Fiscal Commission, but apparently the members could not reconcile the issues in such a way as to satisfy the different economic and political views represented by the members. Nothing came of the effort.[11] In 1956, the

[8] *The Journal of Commerce,* New York, May 30, 1966, p. 1.

[9] Nathan N. Gordon, "The Rule of Tax Treaties," *Taxes and International Business,* National Association of Manufacturers, New York, 1965, p. 16.

[10] *Ibid.*

[11] *Ibid.*

Fiscal Committee of the Organization for European Economic Cooperation was established to study fiscal questions relating to double taxation and other fiscal questions of a similar nature. In its report of 1958, the committee stated that ". . . obstacles represented by double taxation are not, in general, the result of any deliberate intention. Their effect is simply that a person doing business or investing in more than one State is arbitrarily given less favorable treatment than a person who does business or investing in one State alone."[12]

U.S. treaties for avoidance of double taxation. As of mid-1968, the United States had treaties with 26 countries pertaining to the taxation of U.S. business interests abroad and foreign business interests in the United States. These treaties were with:

Country	*Year*
Sweden	1939 (Supplementary 1963 and 1965)
France	1939 (Supplementary 1946, 1948, 1956, 1965, and 1967)
Canada	1942 (Supplementary 1950 and 1956)
United Kingdom	1945 (Supplementary 1946, 1954, 1957, 1958)
Union of South Africa	1946 (Supplementary 1950 and 1952)
Denmark	1948
New Zealand	1948
Netherlands	1948 (Supplementary 1955 and 1963)
Belgium	1948 (Supplementary 1952 and 1957)
Norway	1949 (Suplementary 1958)
Ireland	1949
Greece	1950 (Supplementary 1961)
Switzerland	1951
Finland	1952
Australia	1953
Japan	1954 (Supplementary 1957 and 1960)
Germany	1954
Italy	1955
Honduras	1956
Austria	1956
Luxembourg	1962
Pakistan	1957
Philippines	1964
Brazil	1967

[12] *The Elimination of Double Taxation,* Organization for European Economic Cooperation, Paris, 1958, p. 12.

In addition, treaties that had been negotiated several months before with Israel, Thailand, and the United Arab Republic were awaiting ratification by the Senate. The delay was apparently attributable to the inclusion of a tax-sparing provision in each, which would have treated certain foreign taxes as "paid" for purposes of foreign tax credit, even though the taxes were not imposed by the foreign government as an inducement to investment. The object of these treaties is basically to secure agreement between the country in which the income is earned or the property is located and the country of which the owner is a citizen as to which country has the right to levy taxes in order that the citizen will not be taxed on the same property (including income) in both countries.

There is no absolute uniformity in the conventions to which the United States subscribes. The conventions were negotiated under varying circumstances at different times and with countries whose taxing structures differ widely. They usually specify, however, how the taxes will be imposed and the persons or types of persons to receive benefits. A key feature of the conventions is the concept of "permanent establishment". Normally, the United States and the other country party to the convention agree to exempt from tax, or at least to reduce the tax on, certain types of income earned by persons of the other country if their activity or "economic penetration" *does not* take the form of a permanent establishment. The definition of a permanent establishment is in itself a matter of agreement between the negotiating partners, based on what may be called common business practice. But in general it may be accepted that a branch, factory, or fixed place of business constitutes a permanent establishment and therefore subjects the owners to tax in the country in which located, regardless of their nationality; for foreigners, however, the tax is on income earned in the host country. There is less clarity in agency relationships, but often an establishment is considered permanent if an agent has general authority to negotiate and conclude contracts binding on the principal or if he maintains a stock of merchandise from which he regularly fills orders on behalf of the principal. It is obvious that a company should well consider whether its interest abroad is served through a permanent establishment (this is obviously unavoidable in some cases) ; the legal and physical arrangement for doing such business will determine the status for tax purposes. In some cases, an office used solely for the purchase of merchandise is not considered a permanent establishment; but in others, it is. On the other hand, it seems to be usual that carrying on business through an independent agent or broker does not constitute a permanent establishment. Since the definitions are not uniform, and since tax rates may differ widely (which may render the permanent establishment question academic), one must study the respective tax conventions to reach an informed decision.

A convention typically departs from narrow application of the tax laws by exempting or partially exempting certain types of income from application of the income tax of respective countries. Under U.S. treaties, for example, a U.S. business entity is not subject to tax by the foreign country unless it operates therein with a permanent establishment. Reciprocally, income earned in the United States by foreigners is excluded from U.S. tax if it is earned without the creation of a permanent establishment. For example, a businessman may be in the country for only a few days, staying in a hotel. He does business, however, during the trip—which was its purpose. How is income so earned to be taxed? This exemption does not, or may not, apply to passive or investment income, that is, dividends, interest, rents, and royalties. The conventions to which the United States is a party also specify the manner of treatment of other types of income, such as income from investments, industrial property rights, and transportation profits.

The OECD Draft Double Taxation Convention. As a result of study and discussion by the Fiscal Committee of the Organization for European Economic Cooperation, which later became the OECD Fiscal Committee, there evolved a number of articles which eventually constituted the basis of a Draft Double Taxation Convention on Income and Capital. The draft convention was presented to member states in 1963. As of mid-1968 it is still a draft convention, but the OECD Council has recommended to the governments of member countries that in concluding or revising bilateral conventions between themselves they conform to the draft convention and that multilateral conventions between member states which are also members of regional groupings also conform to the draft convention. The United States has adopted certain of the proposals in its subsequently negotiated conventions.

Among the items covered in the proposed convention are the following:

1. *Determination of fiscal domicile.* This depends on where one lives, works, or is a national.
2. *Definition of permanent establishment.* This is somewhat more liberal than has been adopted in most U.S. conventions, but the United States has now begun to use the modified definition. The principal difference is that permanent establishment, under this definition, does not include:
    a. Maintenance of inventory solely for purposes of storage, display, or delivery.
    b. Maintenance of a stock of goods solely for processing by another enterprise.
    c. Maintenance of a fixed place of business solely for pur-

chasing goods or merchandise, or for collecting information for the enterprise.

3. *Tax jurisdiction of profits from ships and aircraft operating internationally.* Their income is to be taxable only in the country in which effective management of the enterprise is situated.
4. *Allocation of income for tax purposes when arising from non-arm's length arrangements between related companies.* This privilege is to be reserved to each interested signatory.
5. *Dividends.* These are to be taxable in the country of the recipient, except:
   a. The country of source may charge a tax of 5 percent if the recipient is a company owning directly at least 25 percent of the capital of the company paying the dividend.
   b. The country of source may charge a tax of 15 percent of the gross dividends in all other cases.
6. *Interest.* This is to be taxable in the country of the recipient, but the country of source may impose a tax of 10 percent.
7. *Royalties.* These are to be taxable only in the country of the recipient.
8. *Capital gains.* These are to be taxable in the country in which the property is situated.
9. *Income from immovable property.* This is to be taxable in the country in which the property is situated.
10. *Income from personal services.* A distinction is made as to the basis on which the services are rendered, that is, whether it is as an independent professional, for example, or whether the services are the result of dependent employment.

There are a number of areas in which work is continuing toward clarification and technical improvements of this draft convention. The convention is certain to make its influence widely felt as new conventions are written and old ones are revised. For example, the tax treaty between the United States and France, renegotiated in 1967, is based on the model tax treaty designed by the OECD.

One may conclude that the networks of bilateral conventions, and especially the drafting of model tax treaties, will serve to remove barriers to international trade and investment and to render more mobile the international movements of capital and technology as economic factors. The conventions will also be significant factors in decisions regarding the types of business organizations to be established.

TAX SPARING

As a means of inducement to making the investment, some countries have negotiated with the investor temporarily to spare him the imposition of part or all of certain taxes to which he would otherwise be subject. The same practice is found in cities and states in the United States. From the international business viewpoint, there is no advantage to business enterprise in having a tax spared in a foreign country if the income is then taxable at the same or a higher rate in the country of residence or control; there would be such an advantage if the foreign tax rate were higher than in the country of residence. Some countries permit a tax credit for taxes which have been spared abroad, but others, notably the United States, do not; the credit is for taxes *paid* abroad. Another type of tax sparing that affects international business is the practice of rebating certain indirect taxes on goods exported, which taxes would apply if the goods were sold domestically. In the United States, Federal excise taxes are of this type. This is a subject of much concern because of differing tax systems in various countries.

Chapter X

International Monetary Requirements

The international financial mechanism takes care of the *daily* settling of the multitude of international payments and claims. Hopefully, it does so without subjecting the various economies and the economic policy institutions in the several countries to extreme disorderly speculation in the foreign exchange markets. The need is for financing increasing volumes of international business of all types without any major country's abruptly losing or gaining so much in monetary reserves that its internal economic policies must be modified drastically to accommodate to a rather transitory situation. The larger consideration is that governments play a more direct role in the economy than was the case a few decades ago; they wish to pursue certain national economic policies (growth, price stability, and high levels of employment) without severely disrupting harmonious international economic relationships or the expansion of international trade.

Study of the financial mechanism fosters a better understanding of some of the major forces that affect the international business picture—whether the fluctuations be day by day, seasonal, or secular. It also contributes to a better understanding of the forces that bear on the availability and cost of funds to business, domestically as well as internationally.

DIMENSIONS OF THE PROBLEM

In the broad sense, the capability of absorbing foreign trade pressures on national monetary systems is part of the objective of international financial liquidity. Without this resiliency the national monetary and banking systems would be unable to accommodate to the strains of changing volumes (including prices) and directions of world trade requiring financing—and this in the context of a spectacular growth in international trade and payments in the postwar years. A review of these dimensions will indicate just how spectacular this growth has been. Though total payments relate to all types of international transactions, both private and governmental, the major part is connected with trade in merchandise, and reference to these volumes alone will put the problem in perspective. World imports and world exports must closely equate, although the former is a larger amount, statistically, because it includes transportation and insurance charges. Moreover, the financing is needed to pay for imports, not exports. Hence the statistics presented will be primarily those of merchandise imports.

Total world merchandise imports (cost, insurance, and freight) were $192.2 billion in 1966—up from $97.5 billion in 1956. This is an increase of $95 billion in ten years. Now this change is in total dollar volume. As might be expected, the change is not regular from year to year, nor has it been equal in major trading areas (see Exhibits 22 and 23). This suggests that changes in direction as well as in volume have a very substantial part to play in the changing picture of foreign trade and other international transactions to be financed.

Irregular changes in total volume are at times rugged, and while some seasonal patterns may be detected, it is not appropriate to our subject to attempt to demonstrate them now. Instead, a few important short-term changes may be cited (see Exhibit 24).

Aside from the relative importance of individual countries in world trade, which has a bearing on the total volume of a given country's commerce that has to be financed, there are two other aspects, equally and perhaps more important in the short run—the *direction* of trade that has to be financed and the uneven and large changes in export and import volumes for any given country from year to year (and within a year as well). For example, for the United States alone, consider the impact on its monetary system of the receipts of and demands for foreign exchange arising from year-to-year changes in total exports and imports, as shown in Exhibit 25. These are annual aggregates, within which there are substantial irregularities by month and day. In addition there are variations, at times divergent, in our trade with different countries. On a geographic basis, as shown in Exhibit 26, the net changes again emphasize the need for resiliency or for very quick and broad adjustment in the monetary mechanism through which circulates the totality of foreign exchange receipts and demands.

EXHIBIT 22

IMPORTS OF MERCHANDISE, WORLD
($ billion)

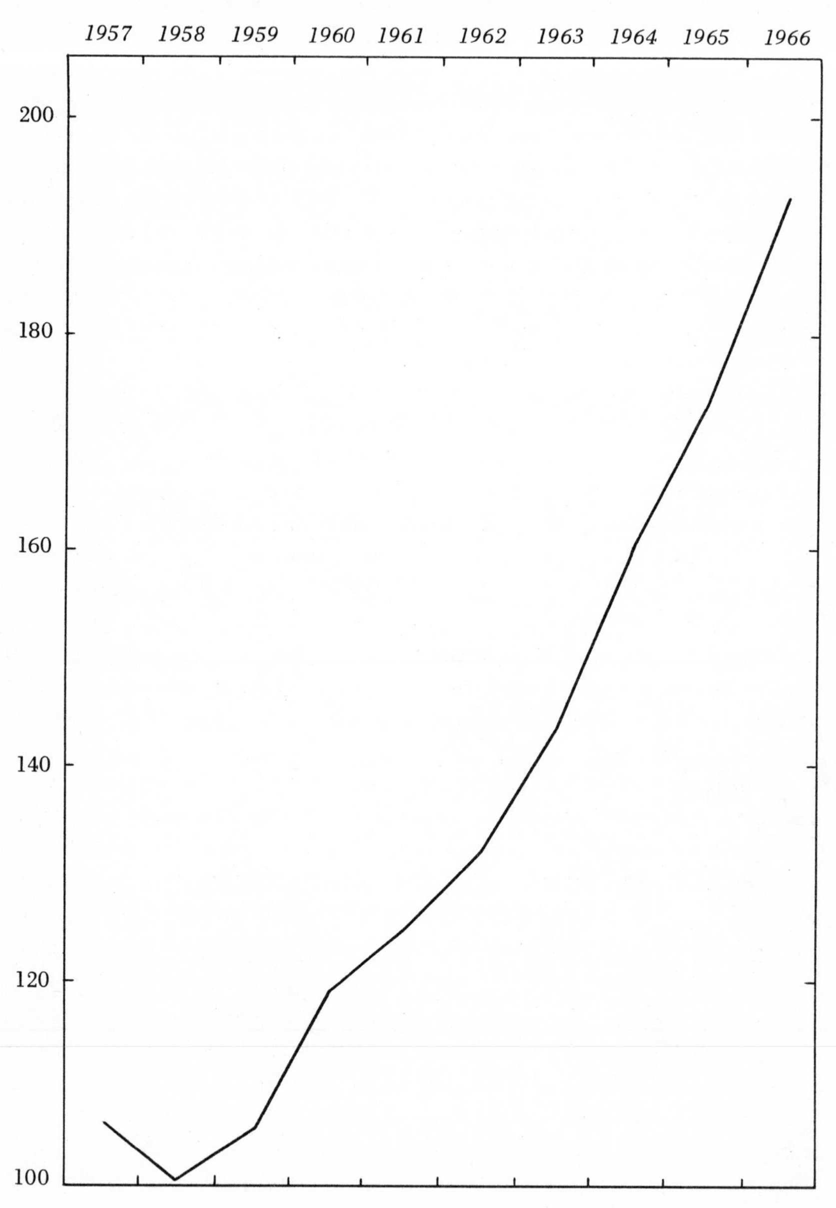

Source: *International Financial Statistics*, International Monetary Fund, Washington, D. C., Supplement to 1966-67 issues, p. xvii; December 1967, p. 35.

EXHIBIT 23

IMPORTS OF MERCHANDISE,
BY SELECTED COUNTRIES AND GROUPINGS
(1956 = 100%)

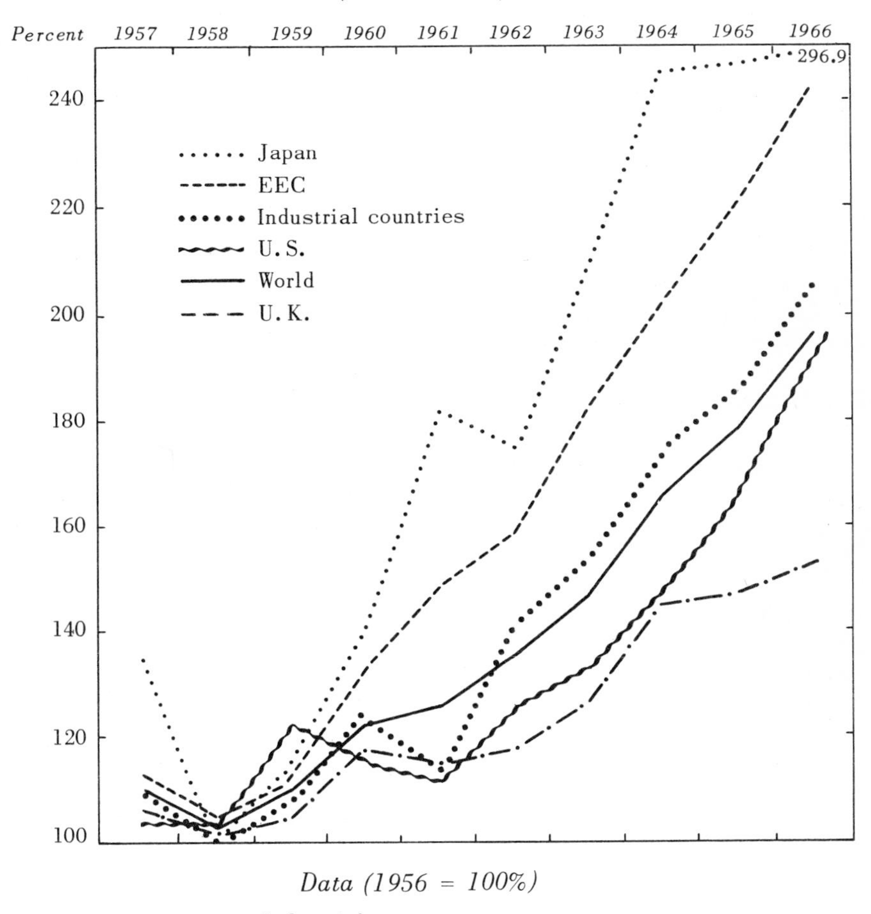

Data (1956 = 100%)

Year	*World*	*Industrial Countries*	*U.S.*	*EEC*	*Japan*	*U.K.*
1957	109.8	108.7	104.3	111.6	134.4	105.5
1958	102.9	100.9	104.3	103.6	93.8	97.3
1959	109.4	109.1	121.4	108.9	112.5	103.6
1960	122.5	123.8	117.1	132.3	140.6	118.2
1961	127.8	114.5	113.6	148.4	181.2	115.5
1962	135.8	140.3	127.1	159.1	175.0	118.2
1963	147.3	153.6	132.1	181.1	209.4	127.3
1964	165.0	172.4	145.0	202.7	246.9	144.5
1965	179.5	187.7	165.9	220.6	256.2	146.4
1966	197.1	206.8	197.8	241.2	296.9	151.8

Source: Developed from *International Financial Statistics*, International Monetary Fund, Washington, D.C., Supplement to 1966-67 issues, p. xvii; December 1967, p. 35.

EXHIBIT 24

SHORT-TERM CHANGES IN SELECTED
WORLD TRADE VOLUMES, 1965 AND 1966
($ million)

	Dollar Change		Percent Change	
World	+	—	+	—
Fourth quarter 1964 to first quarter 1965		7.1		4
First to fourth quarters 1965	23.8		13	
Fourth quarter 1965 to first quarter 1966		1.1		.5
Third to fourth quarters 1965	13.6		8	
Third to fourth quarters 1966	11.7		6	
First to fourth quarters 1966	15.7		6	
United States				
Fourth quarter 1964 to first quarter 1965		1.9		.9
First to fourth quarters 1965	5.6		28	
Fourth quarter 1965 to fourth quarter 1966	3.8		15	

Note: Quarterly figures (in dollars) are expressed at annual rate.

Source: *International Financial Statistics*, May 1967, p. 35.

LIQUIDITY

Few topics, except perhaps the balance of payments situation of the United States, have engaged the attention of international economists and bankers in recent years as much as that of rearranging the international financial mechanism. In fact, this interest has been stimulated by the balance of payments situation because both are part of the larger consideration referred to a short time ago—that is, the desire to pursue certain *national* economic policies without severe disruption to harmonious *international* economic relationships or the expansion of international trade. This is a far cry from the discipline of the gold standard under which domestic policies, such as they were, were fundamentally subordinate to a nation's international obligations and reputation. There was a somewhat more closely knit international economy under it, with the markets playing the major role in adjustments, than under the system which followed it. And, ironically, this is what much of the intergovernmental "cooperation" seeks to achieve today.

Liquidity involves, in substance, the arrangement made between nations concerning the value of each other's currency in terms of others and probably

EXHIBIT 25

U.S. EXPORTS AND IMPORTS
(1956 = 100)

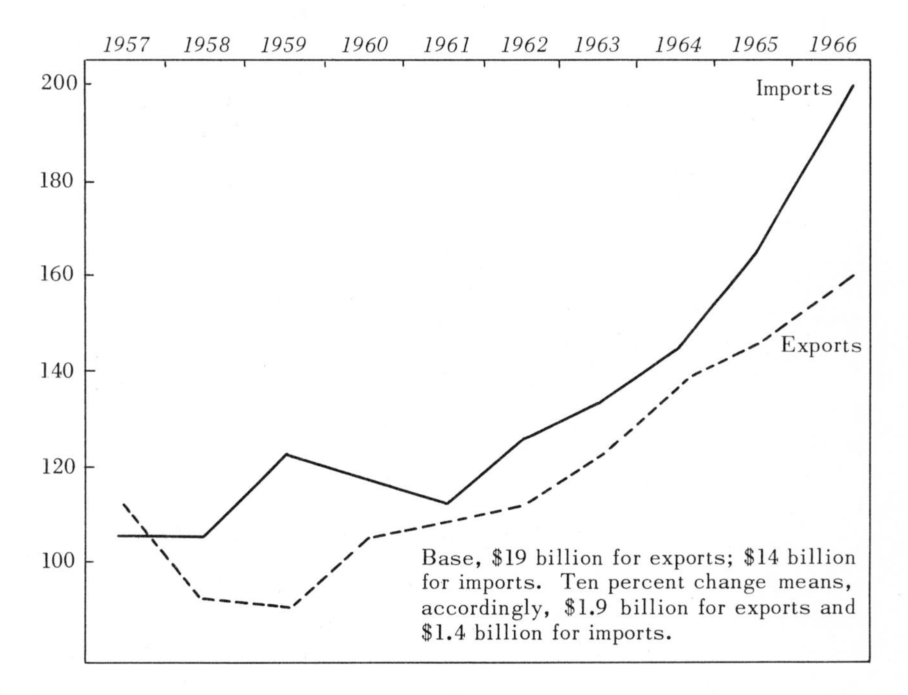

Supporting Data

	Exports		*Imports*	
	$ billion	*Relation to base year*	*$ billion*	*Relation to base year*
1956	19.1	100.0	14.0	100
1957	20.9	109.4	14.6	104.2
1958	17.9	93.7	14.6	104.2
1959	17.6	92.1	17.0	121.4
1960	20.6	107.8	16.4	117.1
1961	21.0	109.9	15.9	113.5
1962	21.7	113.6	17.8	127.1
1963	23.4	122.5	18.6	132.8
1964	26.6	139.2	20.3	145.0
1965	27.5	143.9	34.2	165.7
1966	30.5	159.6	27.7	197.8

Source: *International Financial Statistics*, Supplement to 1966-67 issues, pp. xvi-xvii; and December 1967, p. 35.

EXHIBIT 26

CHANGES IN U.S. EXPORT AND IMPORT VOLUMES, BETWEEN 1965 AND 1966
(With selected areas and countries, in $ million)

Trade With	*Exports*	*Imports*	*Net Change*
Canada	+1,018	+1,293	−275
United Kingdom	+ 122	+ 381	−259
Latin America	+ 447	+ 295	152
Near East	+ 123	+ 12	111
Japan	+ 285	+ 550	−265
Western Europe	+ 589	+1,530	−941

Source: *Overseas Business Reports*, U.S. Department of Commerce, Washington, D. C., 67-43, August 1967.

in terms of a common denominator, such as gold; arrangements for the interchange of such currencies with the least possible governmental interference—that is, with the greatest degree of unrestricted convertibility; and the establishment of institutions necessary to accommodate to increasing and variable demands for foreign exchange.

Several proposals have been made in the last ten years to modify the arrangements in force since the end of World War II. That there is no solid agreement among the leading spokesmen—bankers, academicians, government officials, and the business press—is evident from the voluminous literature on the subject, especially in the early 1960's. Substantially, all are in agreement that something must be done, but the questions are "what?" and "when?"

The nature of liquidity. Just as individuals face a problem of keeping on hand enough cash (which earns nothing) or quickly realizable investments (convertible into cash on one or a few days' notice) to finance their varying needs and opportunities, and just as the domestic financial mechanism faces the need for being able to provide funds—sometimes in quickly changing volumes and with volatile intensity of demand—so must the institutions of the international financial structure contemplate a certain liquidity. For the confidence on which a credit system is based rests solely on the faith that the personal or institutional debtor will be able and willing to pay on demand or at maturity of the investment—that is, that there will be a scheduled or optional (to the creditor) conversion into cash and that the schedule will be honored. Paying, in this context, means in good, usable, convertible money; and if in a foreign currency, then in a currency that can be converted into the creditor's own national currency without loss. This is a serious problem to individuals, who stand to suffer personal loss, and to officials of private institutions or governments, who are, in fact, trustees of other people's money.

Possibly because of mutual exposure to the same dangers, in varying degrees of uncontrollability because they are rooted in a multiude of personal decisions by private citizens, there appears to be a tolerance and an understanding—in fact, cooperation—among government officials which are not observable between private creditors and debtors. This could be, also, because private citizens may not have access to as wide a range of current intelligence or because they do not have to consider the balanced impact on their individual actions.

When a person speaks of *international* liquidity, he does not refer to convertibility of earnings or claims abroad into cash or into coin of the realm with which expenses or obligations incurred domestically can be settled. This aspect of liquidity is primarily of interest to private citizens domestically. Rather, the reference is to convertibility into something which itself can be used now or later in settling a *nation's* aggregate obligations, public and private, to foreigners, public and private.[1] The "something" into which foreign currency received is expected to be convertible, if desired, is generally gold or some asset agreed to among governments as being as "good as gold"—that is, something useful for monetary reserves domestically and acceptable as well in the conduct of international business—in the "settlement" of international payments. There is, of course, no net settlement, ever, in total. The only things finally settled are individual transactions or obligations. *International* liquidity, then, is concerned with the coverage of transfers among governments or governmental institutions (treasuries, central banks, or private banks authorized to deal in foreign exchange) which themselves will have become the residual holders of certain claims against foreign economies through the aggregate effect of the markets' settling the multitude of daily individual transactions.

But this means that because of the aggregate of transactions, private and public, nations will lose or gain in gold and monetary reserves. A significant change in the volume of reserves available calls for corrective action by the

[1] This does not mean that it actually will be used in final settlement; the provision pending actual balancing out by private transactions may simply be a temporary "arrangement" as between governments and/or central banks in lieu of a loss of gold or actual monetary reserve.

market (the exchange rate, interest rates, and/or prices of goods) or by the government (its economic policy and programs).

Liquidity rests, as just stated, on monetary reserves; and the concept of adequacy of liquidity rests not on the volume of world trade, but on the relationship of reserves to the size and duration of anticipated deficits in a nation's international accounts. Deficits or surpluses there will always be—except in strict barter. The question is how much tolerance there should be before corrective action is *forced,* and whether reserves are adequate to finance this "tolerance."

Considerations of liquidity also involve a distinction between legal and operating reserves and between official and private reserves. Both "legal" and "official" refer to government and central bank holdings in the case of international finance. They consist primarily of gold, but many include certain foreign exchange—that is, claims on other countries or on international institutions. Operating reserves available to governments and central banks are far broader. They include not only gold and foreign exchange but a variety of credit arrangements, some of very recent origin, designed to conserve the use of gold.

It helps, finally, to distinguish between official and private international financial resources. Official resources consist of the holdings of governments and central banks; private resources of the holdings of businesses and commercial banks and others in the market. Major emphasis in assessing the adequacy of international liquidity must be placed on *official* monetary reserves, with little attention given to comparable assets in the hands of private holders. These latter are important sources of financing and of commercial liquidity internationally; and, in fact, they normally constitute the reservoir of funds actually used in the settlement of international business transactions. But they belong to private owners and not to governments. Law or decree would be necessary to bring them into government hands. Moreover, official holdings are not directly used to make payments for the multitude of individual international transactions. Rather, ". . . official holdings of international monetary reserves provide the means whereby the monetary authorities of a country experiencing a balance of payments deficit may support its currency in the foreign exchange markets until payments equilibrium is restored."[2]

Consistent with this broader view of working or operating reserves, the following definition of liquidity was used by the Federal Reserve Bank of New York in its *Monthly Review* of November 1963:[3]

[2] Roy L. Reierson, *The Question of International Liquidity,* Bankers Trust Company, New York, 1965, p. 10.

[3] P. 167.

> World liquidity, as understood in this context, refers to the generally accepted official means of settling imbalances in international payments. Thus it comprises the gold and foreign exchange holdings of monetary authorities, plus such additional means of payment as may be available to them through international and bilateral credit facilities.

This definition properly brings in the International Monetary Fund and some other formal arrangements or institutions comprising the international monetary system.

The measure of liquidity. Because of the different elements or "assets" that can be called monetary reserves, there is no agreed and final definition of international liquidity and no satisfactory measure of it. Nor can one say with precision that there is, in the final sense, adequate liquidity any more than one can say, in the ultimate sense, that there is adequate water in a reservoir. The question of adequacy depends on contemplated usage and on anticipated replenishment, and even on alternate or emergency sources. Should either be far off the projected mark, the "normal" adequacy could be inadequate or considerably excessive.

Depending on the definition adopted, one may attempt to "measure" liquidity in the narrower sense mainly by statistics on official monetary reserves. Certain parts of this aggregate are easily measurable as, for example, monetary gold and the IMF gold tranche.[4] But certain other parts are not, since one nation's international liability must of necessity be some other nation's asset. It appears that attempting to measure world liquidity of this nature and then comparing the results with some other variable, such as world imports, is at best only an exercise in tying together the facts that international transactions must be paid for and that the way in which balance of payments deficits or surpluses are carried (wherein settlement is deferred) has implications for other countries.

Nevertheless, the measurable components of reserves, such as appear to indicate international liquidity in the International Financial Statistics of the International Monetary Fund, are shown in Exhibits 27 and 28. They show a total growth of about 23 percent since 1958, with gold proportionately declining in importance, offset by increases in holdings of foreign exchange and reserve positions in the fund. The increase in foreign exchange is derived mainly from increased claims on the United States and the United Kingdom.

As indicated, these total reserves cannot properly be related to some other statistic, such as the volume of world trade, in order to assess their

[4] "Gold tranche" means that portion of a member's quota paid to IMF in gold. Drawing rights, up to that amount, are unconditional.

EXHIBIT 27

GOLD, RESERVE POSITIONS IN FUND, AND FOREIGN EXCHANGE HOLDINGS OF MONETARY AUTHORITIES
($ billion)

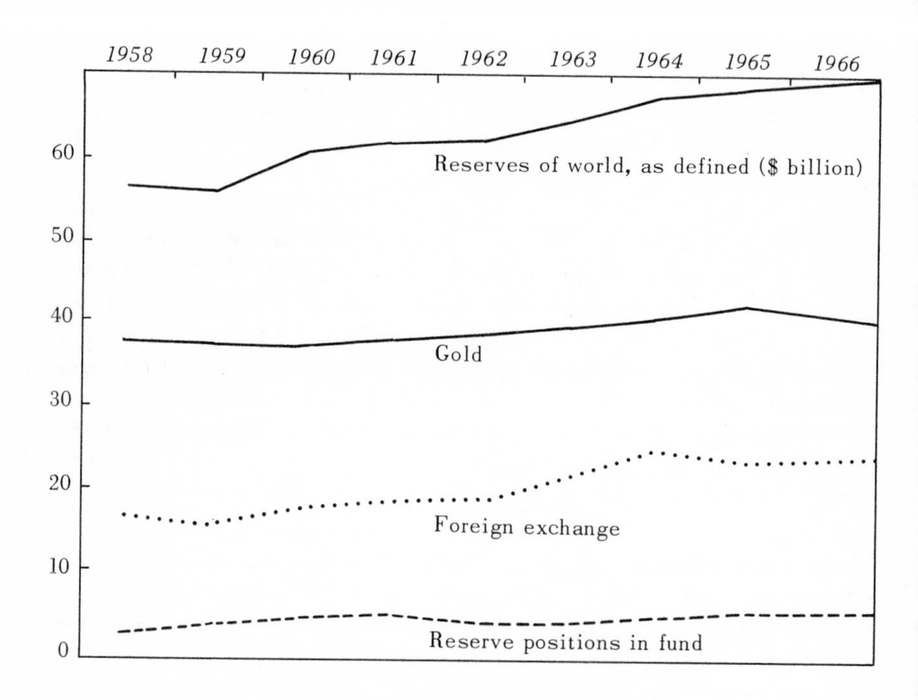

Supporting Data: In $ Billion

Year	*Gold*	*Reserve Positions in Fund*	*Foreign Exchange*	*Total*
1958	38.0	2.6	17.0	57.6
1959	37.9	3.3	16.2	57.4
1960	38.0	3.6	18.7	60.3
1961	38.8	4.2	19.3	62.3
1962	39.3	3.8	19.8	62.9
1963	40.2	3.9	22.1	66.2
1964	40.8	4.2	23.5	68.5
1965	41.9	5.4	23.0	70.3
1966	40.4	6.2	23.7	70.3

Source: *International Financial Statistics*, December 1966, p. 15; November 1967, p. 16

EXHIBIT 28

MAIN MONETARY RESERVE COMPONENTS OF WORLD GOLD, RESERVE POSITIONS IN FUND, AND OFFICIAL FOREIGN EXCHANGE HOLDINGS

(In percent of total)

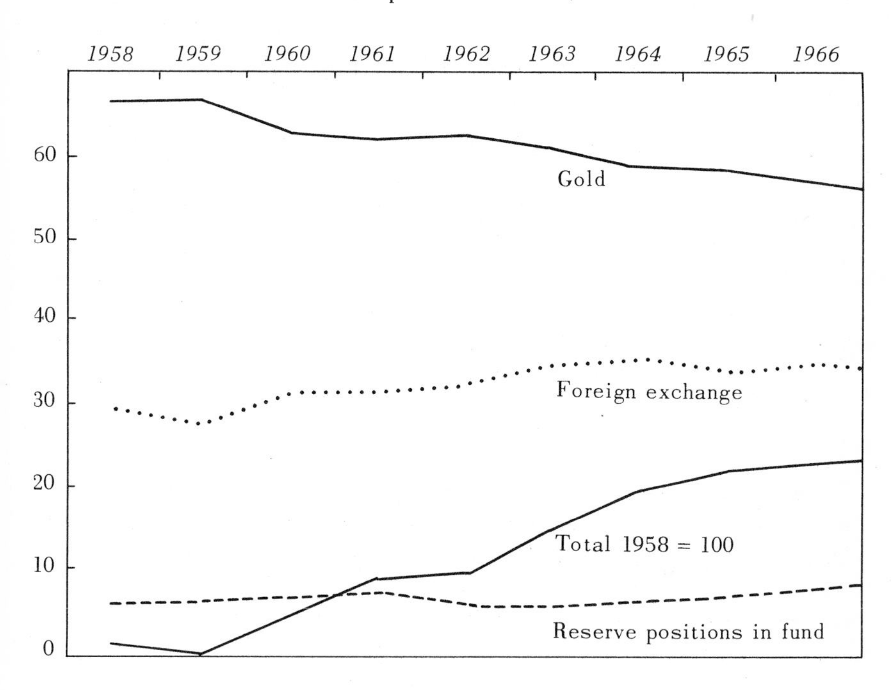

Supporting Data: Percent of Total

Year	*Gold*	*Reserve Positions in Fund*	*Foreign Exchange*	*Total*
1958	66.0	4.4	29.5	100.0
1959	66.0	5.6	28.2	99.5
1960	63.1	5.9	30.9	104.7
1961	62.4	6.6	30.9	108.2
1962	62.6	6.0	31.3	108.9
1963	60.8	5.9	33.2	114.8
1964	59.6	6.0	34.3	118.9
1965	59.6	7.6	32.7	121.9
1966	57.1	8.8	34.0	124.3

Source: *International Financial Statistics*, December 1966, p. 15; November 1967, p. 16.

exact adequacy or deficiency. This is because they are not used in the settlement of the actual multitude of individual transactions. What monetary authorities are concerned with, therefore, is not that there is *enough* in the way of funds to *finance* overall private business transactions. This is no real problem. The fundamental point is that they are concerned with the ability of an *individual* country's monetary authorities to meet the stresses and strains of financing the total of its international transactions without having to take one of the following measures:

- Interpose overly depressing restrictions on the volume of such transactions.
- Subject the domestic economy to overly restrictive or deflationary policies.
- Break the value of its established foreign exchange rate by more than the tolerance allowed under the International Monetary Fund Agreement.

Perhaps it would bring the picture into better focus if we think in terms of aggregates. Instead of billions of persons, there are 130 or so countries doing business with each other, each with a national currency to which the domestic economy is geared. Now if trade alone or total transactions were to be equally balanced as between outgo and intake in a given period for each country, consistent with credit-settlement terms, then one would carry the other and there would be no problem. But, as shown earlier, total volume changes; prices change; the direction of trade changes; and different types of goods move under different credit terms. The result is that any country's money may be under attack from one or more other currencies, depending on how total transactions are going among countries. Such attack may and will come from several quarters, and its origin may actually have no relation to a country's bilateral trading patterns. As an example, the pressure on the U.S. dollar in recent years has not been because of the movement of our commerce with any one country or region, but because of our overall position.

SIGNIFICANCE OF THE INTERNATIONAL FINANCIAL MECHANISM TO INTERNATIONAL BUSINESS

Even though most *international* financial institutions are not of immediate and direct concern to international business, they are, nevertheless, of very substantial underlying significance. This is because they establish and contribute to the environment in which international business can and must be conducted. Without them, many private business decisions would be impeded because of an added element of uncertainty in the environment. One may say, then, that one of the greatest contributions such institutions make is to bring forth a climate of greater certainty so that decisions and plans can be undertaken more confidently. This observation derives from three functions or objectives of such institutions.

Maintenance of stable exchange rates. If there were not some basis for expecting that the price of foreign exchange (the exchange rate) in 30 days, 90 days, 6 months, or 1 year from now—and perhaps even longer— would be close to what it is today, or at least reasonably and definitely determinable, decisions affecting both trade and investment or licensing would be more difficult to arrive at; and this should result in a diminution of orderly international business. Certainly, long-term contracts for commodities or long-term credits for capital goods would tend to be more risky. Investment and licensing decisions would be affected because of greater uncertainty as to the rate at which dividends, interest, and royalties could be converted. Stability of international rates is similar to being able to use the same money within one nation. Of course, one may say that the prudent act is to cover the forward position by hedging. But hedging is possible in only a very few currencies; a futures market does not exist in all currencies.

It must also be recognized that there is a strong sentiment among some academicians that exchange rates should be fully flexible—that is, not tied down to gold or to the dollar. The rates of exchange should be allowed to find their level each day, presumably without much government interference, if any. That this would cause some rather severe and sharp adjustments in prices of goods is indeed a possibility and, in fact, one of the advantages claimed for the theory. Whether governments would be willing to forgo their present active role in foreign exchange markets is doubtful, however. But it is an interesting thought and a fundamental consideration in the question of liquidity and the need for international monetary reserves at all.

Quantitative monetary reserve assistance to individual countries. This assistance enables individual countries to shield themselves against unduly abrupt changes in and pressures on their reserve positions. By so doing, they may avoid or at least postpone severe dislocations in their domestic economies and in domestic economic and social programs. This shielding is, of course, only temporary, but it does buy time within which gradual and moderate, or controlled, corrective policies may be undertaken.

Some prospect of economic stability is clearly an important element in investment or licensing decisions—for example, it can render one country more attractive than another—and in the timing, volume, and financial arrangements of private export and import transactions. Hence the availability of liquid resources in case of need, enabling a nation to follow less drastic policies should its international transactions be in deficit, is important to private business in its marketing and investment decisions.

Special assistance, quantitative and qualitative, to developing countries. Two characteristics of many developing countries are: first, their dependence on one or two major commodities for export earnings, the volumes and prices of which may fluctuate widely over a season; and, second, their desire and need for economic development. Naturally, development is not accomplished in a short time, so longer-term planning and financing are necessary. Arrangement has been made by IMF, via compensatory financing, to meet the needs of developing countries for greater certainty as to their access to foreign exchange. But the conditions of access to this special financing and the conditions of repayment require that the developing countries justify their needs and objectives more clearly before international forums. This may be looked on as qualitative assistance as well as quantitative. For international business to know that country *X* has this facility and that its plans and policies (which intelligent business must follow as one guide to marketing or investing in that country) are being subjected to closer intergovernmental scrutiny is a plus factor in arriving at a decision on credit terms and on methods of financing as well as on pricing. In a monograph by Joseph Gold, general counsel of the International Monetary Fund,[5] emphasis is placed on the obligations of good conduct that are legally binding on member states, on the international control of exchange rates, on the avoidance of exchange restrictions, and on the avoidance of discriminatory currency arrangements as being of substantial interest and benefit to international business.

In sum, international financial resources—international liquidity—available to governments or to their central banks buy time for the nation by providing a sort of cushion which absorbs the stresses and strains arising from the settlement of international transactions of all types. The relationship between international liquidity and the domestic credit condition is indirect. If a country loses reserves through international transactions and has little in the way of liquidity facilities to fall back on, its monetary officials may sooner or later need to follow a restrictive credit policy that may reduce the availability and increase the cost of credit obtainable on the domestic market. Such action may have a depressing effect on prices, volume, and employment, and that may reduce the profitability of business.

[5] Joseph Gold, *The International Monetary Fund and Private Business Transactions,* International Monetary Fund, Washington, D.C., 1965.

Chapter XI

International Financial Institutions

Despite recurring criticisms of the gold standard, largely because of the discipline arising from economic and speculative market pressures that it imposes on governments, and of the gold-exchange standard, which presents an inflationary bias, and despite the fact that the ownership of gold except in rather narrowly defined circumstances is illegal for private citizens in the United States and a few other countries, gold still serves as an important binding element in what constitutes the fundamental international monetary institution, the International Monetary Fund (IMF). Internationally, gold is one of the reserve elements used by many central banks and, more importantly, one of the components that must be paid into the International Monetary Fund by members in subscribing their quotas. Moreover, IMF members are required to state the value of their currencies in terms of gold or U.S. dollars; this in turn sets the relative par values of currencies in terms of each other and, since the dollar price of gold is fixed, establishes a reasonably effective price for gold in terms of the respective currencies. Currency prices are kept relatively stable because members are obligated to maintain the market value of their currencies within 1 percent of the established par value by entry into the market as buyers or sellers of foreign exchange.

THE INTERNATIONAL MONETARY FUND

The most important international financial institution in existence, the fund is an independent, specialized organization which has entered into an agreement with the United Nations defining the ways in which these bodies will cooperate in matters of mutual interest. Membership is open to any country willing to subscribe to the Articles of Agreement and to the conditions of membership laid down by the fund—for example, quotas and gold subscriptions and the designation of a fixed rate of exchange. As of mid-1968, there were 107 IMF members.

In substance, IMF consists of a pool of gold and currencies contributed by member countries, their respective quotas being based on their economic size and world trading activity. The fund is designed to make foreign exchange available to countries that have not earned it and which, without such assistance from the fund, might be pressured into following economic policies harmful to their own prosperity or potentially damaging to other countries. It is a specialized agency of the United Nations, designed to promote and aid in the realization of international monetary cooperation. One of its purposes is the promotion of exchange stability and the avoidance of competitive depreciation.

The fund functions in two essential ways. The first of these involves consultations and policy statements. The former are designed to keep the fund well informed so that it can respond quickly to members' requests about dealings in currencies; the latter communicate the fund's attitudes to member countries. The second essential way in which the fund acts is through transactions in foreign exchange and gold. Currency operations are limited in general by the Articles of Agreement to ". . . transactions for the purpose of supplying a member, on the initiative of such member, with the currency of another member in exchange for gold or for the currency of the member desiring to make the purchase."[1]

The member desiring to purchase another's currency must represent to the fund that such currency is needed for making payments which are consistent with provisions of the Articles of Agreement. The member must not have been declared ineligible to use the fund's resources, and the fund's holdings of the currency desired must not have been declared "scarce" by the fund. Quantitative limitations on the proposed purchase are related to the member's quota and the fund's holdings of the member's currency. A member's purchases of foreign exchange (another member's money) from the fund are called "drawings."

In principle, the sum total of the fund's resources does not change materially, except as operations result in profits or losses, as members enter or resign, or as quotas are changed. But the composition of the fund's resources will change by the process of any member's buying the currency of another and paying for such currency with its own or with gold, by the proc-

[1] Article V, Section 2.

ess of repurchasing its currency with convertible currency or with gold, or by the process of selling its currency to the fund for gold.[2]

Repurchase arrangements. When a member government purchases another's currency and pays for it with its own, it undertakes an obligation to repurchase its own currency, which may be done either with a convertible currency or with gold. The obligation does not hold if the requisite amount of that member's currency has been purchased from IMF by another, and terms of the obligation are hedged with references to monetary reserves of the member and to fund quotas.

The total of the original quotas of countries represented at the Bretton Woods, New Hampshire, conference in 1945 was $8,800 million, of which the U.S. quota was $2,750 million.[3] But by June 30, 1947, following ratification of the agreement and establishment of par values, total *subscriptions* to the fund amounted to $6,535 million. Through increases in quotas, accession of additional members, and withdrawals from membership, subscribed quotas in succeeding years were as follows:[4]

1948	$ 7,976 million
1953	$ 8,738 million
1958	$ 9,193 million
1963	$15,560 million
1967	$20,891 million
1968 (February)	$21,037 million

During this time there were two general increases in member quotas for the purpose of increasing the fund's resources: by 50 percent in 1959 and by 25 percent in 1966. Subsequent to this, further discussions have dealt with the possibility of further increases in fund resources and with changes in the manner of availability of such resources to members. As of early 1968, the respective quotas ranged from $5,160 million for the United States to $5 million for Gambia. About ten other countries, mainly in Africa, had quotas of less than $10 million each.

As a procedural adjunct to transactions in exchange, the fund has adopted two policies that are designed to aid members in their policy planning. One is *standby arrangements;* the other is *compensatory financing.* Under

[2] Article VII, Section 2 (ii) provides that the fund may require a member to sell its currency for gold (in effect, the fund sells gold) to replenish the fund's holdings of that member's (scarce) currency.

[3] Quotas are subject to change by fund decision. The U.S.S.R. quota agreed to at Bretton Woods was $1,200 million, but that nation did not subscribe to membership.

[4] *International Financial Statistics,* International Monetary Fund, Washington, D.C., May 1967, p. 8.

the former, which came into being in 1952, members may enter into arrangements with the fund ". . . to assure that drawings may be made up to specified limits." In effect, standby arrangements are lines of credit, negotiated in advance of actual use, that spell out the specific policies which the member has indicated it intends to pursue in the exchange, monetary, and fiscal fields. Most fund drawings are against standby arrangements.[5] As of early 1968, formal standby arrangements had been made with 26 countries, all of which were either small, or developing, or both.[6]

The second policy, *compensatory financing,* was adopted to assist developing countries which are heavily dependent on a few commodities for export earnings. The pattern of earnings in such cases is apt to be irregular and subject to sharp changes. The arrangement, as described by the fund, is as follows:

> Members that experience an export shortfall may draw under special provisions. A member may make drawings amounting in total to as much as 50 percent of quota to compensate for shortfalls in export proceeds below the medium-term trend (the estimated five-year moving average centered on the shortfall year) with the qualification that outstanding drawings under this provision may not increase by more than 25 percent of quota within any 12-month period. Such drawings must be repaid under the rules that apply to ordinary drawings. . . .[7]

Borrowing arrangements. Because the fund's resources are limited and may at times be inadequate to meet excessive and emergency demands, the fund and the main industrial countries of the world entered into General Arrangements to Borrow in 1962. Under this plan, the countries undertake to lend to the fund specified amounts of their currencies (aggregating to the equivalent of $6 billion), if supplementary resources are needed to forestall or cope with an impairment of the international monetary system. Generally speaking, amounts lent to the fund are repayable when the member whose drawing was financed repurchases its currency from the fund or when the lending country itself experiences a balance of payments deficit. In any event, they are repayable in five years. The General Arrangements to Borrow were first used in December 1964 to finance part of the United Kingdom's drawing of that date.[8]

Special Drawing Rights (SDR). Next to the International Monetary

[5] *Ibid.,* p. 7.
[6] *Ibid.,* April 1968, p. 7.
[7] *Ibid.,* May 1968, p. 6.
[8] *Ibid.,* p. 9.

Fund, itself, perhaps the most exciting development in international finance in many decades was the arrangement negotiated in late 1967 to provide for the deliberate and regulated *creation* of internationally (intergovernmentally) acceptable monetary reserves. These take the form of drawing rights in a special account set up on the books of the International Monetary Fund under internationally agreed conditions. The rationale for this system, within the context of expanding world trade and payments, is based on four points. First, international trade and payments are growing faster than the supply of gold, the most basic reserve. Further, the availability of gold for monetary purposes is erratic, unpredictable, and conditioned by factors other than world trade needs. Second, the next most basic reserve, the gold tranches in the International Monetary Fund, is a fixed amount and could change only as quotas are changed or as the manner of subscribing to established quotas is changed. Third, the use of a single nation's currency as a reserve currency, under the gold-exchange standard procedure, is heavily dependent on the policies of that country; it is unpredictable because of the often conflicting pressures of domestic as against international considerations. Moreover, the increasing availability of such reserves depends on the running of a balance of payments deficit by the key currency country. This may be untenable politically as well as unacceptable economically, with both domestic and international pressures and demands for correction of the imbalance in payments. Fourth, ad hoc arrangements, such as the General Arrangements to Borrow and the central bank swap networks, are just that—ad hoc. Their continuance must be renegotiated periodically, and their absolute availability when demanded may not be assured in all circumstances. Within this context, the search over several years was for a type of reserve which would meet several requirements. First, its amount could be regulated by intergovernmental action. Second, its availability and overall amount could be assured by virtue of its creation through international fiat. Third, its acceptability would be insured by solemn obligation on the part of governments to accept and hold the new type of currency, when offered, according to prescribed procedure. Finally, its use by individual nations would be unconditional.

The SDR facility, as adopted, is an amendment to the IMF Articles of Agreement. It does not contemplate for its purposes any addition to IMF quotas. Nor does its activation call for nations to pay their currencies into a special fund of some sort. Rather, the governments that agreed to the SDR facility undertook the responsibility of accepting Special Drawing Rights from other nations' accounts for use as part of their operating (not necessarily "legal") monetary reserves; Special Drawing Rights would be acquired in exchange for their own currencies. For example, if the United States, exercising its right to the facility, desired German marks, the German Government would have agreed in advance to make marks available in exchange for the SDR allocation of the United States. The former SDR claim of the United States on IMF would then become an IMF obligation to Germany—that is, an asset of Germany's. However, since it could use the Special Drawing Rights to acquire other desired currencies, Germany would be less inclined to demand gold from the United States. Moreover, the Special Drawing Rights accepted by creditor countries would earn a modest return, and therefore holding them would be rendered more attractive financially. The country drawing on its account must pay the interest. The desirability of Special Drawing Rights as assets is buttressed by the requirement that repayment of drawings (reconstitution of the facility, as it is called) is *scheduled* under the SDR agreement. Member countries acquiring other currencies through the SDR facility are obligated to reconstitute their respective positions by paying back into the fund such an amount as would bring the average use over the preceding five-year period to no more than 70 percent of the country's cumulative allocation of drawing rights. Repayment (reconstitution) is to be made effective through turning back convertible currencies to IMF, thus replenishing the currency equivalent of funds drawn out earlier. Willingness to accept Special Drawing Rights from other countries, to the extent called for in the agreement, is further encouraged by the provision in the agreement (Article VI, Section B) that Special Drawing Rights accepted by a participating country are subject to an absolute maintenance of gold value or to provisions similar to Article IV, Section 8.

Referring now to the objectives of such an arrangement as outlined above, the SDR facility is established solely by intergovernmental agreement and IMF action. No money is paid into IMF to get it started. Instead, when it is decided that an allocation be established (the countries having already agreed in advance to accept each other's checks against the allocated accounts) IMF credits each country for the amount of its allocation, which depends on the country's IMF quota. For this reason, the arrangement is sometimes referred to as "paper gold" or "instant gold," which is usable—as gold would be—in settling international accounts, but that does not have to be physically mined or bought on the open market. However, Special Drawing Rights are linked to gold in some degree. In addition to the gold-value guarantee, the surplus countries are expected among themselves to retain Special Drawing Rights in somewhat reasonably comparable proportions as between gold, Special Drawing Rights, and other reserves they acquire. Special Drawing Rights are therefore expected to serve as a supplement to gold.

The amount so allocated in total is to be determined by intergovernmental consultation, taking into account the needs of international trade and payments and the availability of other forms of acceptable reserves, worldwide.

The object is not to create such reserves for the benefit of one or two countries, as their balances of payment may go into deficit, but to bring into the picture an entirely new source of international funds, which rests, by prior agreement on intergovernmental willingness to receive and hold. Special Drawing Rights are based on credit, in a fashion, to the extent that the countries expect the drawers of such rights to repay them in part via the reconstitution process. However, their accessibility to individual countries is automatic and unconditional and does not depend on negotiation with other countries or with IMF. The countries are nevertheless bound by rules which are designed to prevent abuse.

When activated, Special Drawing Rights are essentially book entries; they come into being only after 85 percent of the voting power in IMF approves. Approval means that the countries decide how much of an increase in international reserve is needed and when it will be available. No such arrangements had been made through mid-1968, as the overall arrangement had not been finally approved. Legislative action was needed to ratify amendment of the Articles of Agreement of IMF, and it was expected that such action could not be taken before late 1968 or perhaps 1969. Thereafter, actual activation of the account (by 85 percent of the vote) would have to await a global consensus that liquidity growth in the conventional forms is proceeding too slowly and that the international economy needs these additional credits in order to lift the burden of constriction from a number of countries.

The key point of this arrangement, stressed by most students of the facility, is that it is a deliberate and usable reserve creation. It marks the first time that governments have acted in concert to create a mechanism for generating what could well be permanent additions to world monetary reserve assets. This *creation* is not unmarked by fears, however. This aspect of the problem is well expressed by David R. Francis in the following lines: "The Special Drawing Rights will be based entirely on faith. It is doubtful that they will match gold for many years in attractiveness to central bankers. If not abused through undisciplined issue, faith in them could grow and the importance of gold decline. If abused, Special Drawing Rights would become the Free World's printing-press money, causing global inflation."[9]

THE BANK FOR INTERNATIONAL SETTLEMENTS

One of the first truly international financial institutions still extant is the Bank for International Settlements, located in Basle, Switzerland. It was founded in 1930 by the central banks of seven countries—five European

[9] *Business Abroad,* October 30, 1957, pp. 14–15.

countries, the United States, and Japan.[10] Its statutes (Article 3) describe its purpose in part as follows: "To promote the cooperation of central banks and to provide additional facilities for international financial operations; and to act as trustee or agent in regard to international financial settlements entrusted to it under agreements with the parties concerned." As conditions changed, some of its earlier functions ceased to be of major importance and new ones were assumed.

A prime motive in forming the bank was to facilitate the payment of reparations by Germany, due from the settlement of World War I. The bank continues to serve as fiscal agent of the trustees for certain bonds issued by the Federal Republic of Germany in 1953 and related to German external loans dating back to 1924 and 1930. A second major motive was to encourage cooperation among central banks; this function continues through periodic consultations to prevent conflicts of monetary policy. More recently, an important function has been the bank's acting as agent for the European Monetary Agreement (successor to the European Payments Union, which was one of the features of the Organization for European Economic Cooperation) and serving in a fiduciary capacity for secured loans of the European Coal and Steel Community.

While the bank has extended credits to banks in various countries and is a partner in swap networks of the Federal Reserve (see following section) and of those of certain other central banks, the actual extension of credit does not seem to be or to have been its main accomplishment—at least in the context of significance to international business. Rather, this credit goes to the development of a program of consultation and cooperation among central banks looking toward international financial stability. More recently, in fact for some years, it has enjoyed favor because of its outstanding research and comments on world economic and monetary conditions and its assistance to newer and smaller central banks.[11]

The bank has a capital of 500 million gold francs (about 4.3 francs to the dollar), of which 25 percent is paid up. It deals only with central banks and confines its lending activities to short-term credits.[12]

CENTRAL BANK SWAP NETWORK

As a result of its balance of payments situation and the fact that the dollar is a key currency—that is, it is held as reserve by many countries in lieu

[10] The United States has never subscribed to its originally assigned quota, although Federal Reserve officials participate in consultations among central bankers. Japan has ceased to be a member.

[11] Richard Ward, *International Finance,* Prentice-Hall, Inc., Englewood Cliffs, 1965, p. 107.

[12] John Parke Young, *The International Economy,* The Ronald Press Company, New York, 1963, p. 660.

of their demanding gold—it became necessary to take extra precautionary measures in 1962 to protect the U.S. gold reserves in the event of sudden pressures. This was accomplished by negotiation of a system of Federal Reserve Reciprocal Currency Arrangements, commonly known as the swap network.

Under this arrangement, the Federal Reserve and the central banks of other countries enter into an agreement whereby, in case of need, they are able to draw on each other up to prearranged equivalent amounts. The arrangements constitute standby credits, to be drawn upon as needed. The Federal Reserve Bank of New York called it a move to ". . . create a first line of defense against disorderly speculation in the foreign exchange markets."[13] This means that on the basis of a telephoned or cabled message, the Federal Reserve Bank of New York and its counterparts have immediately available to them additional foreign resources to help in meeting strong selling or buying pressures that, in the eyes of authorities, are basically speculative and disruptive and not fundamentally rooted in underlying business transactions. Since these institutions must work together, continuous and close consultation among all the treasuries and central banks concerned has avoided any conflicts of policy or operations within the group as a whole.

The Federal Reserve swap network, initially arranged with seven banks and the Bank for International Settlements (BIS), and amounting in total to $700 million, had been extended to a total of 14 central banks and the BIS as of September 1968. Total commitments amounted to $9,955 million, as follows:[14]

FEDERAL RESERVE RECIPROCAL CURRENCY ARRANGEMENTS

Other Party to Agreement	*Amount ($ million)*
Austrian National Bank	100
National Bank of Belgium	225
Bank of Canada	1,000
Bank for International Settlements	1,600
Bank of England	2,000
Bank of France	700
National Bank of Denmark	100
German Federal Bank	1,000
Bank of Italy	750
Bank of Japan	1,000
Bank of Mexico	130

[13] *Monthly Review,* Federal Reserve Bank of New York, October 1962, p. 131.
[14] Source: *Ibid.,* March 1966, p. 48; September 1968, p. 179.

Netherlands Bank	400
Bank of Norway	100
Bank of Sweden	250
Swiss National Bank	600

Thus if strong selling pressure against the dollar develops, which might cause fears that the United States is unable to sustain its par value, and which might thus cause or threaten a substantial increase in demands to convert dollar holdings into gold or substantial offerings of dollars at lower prices than par, the Federal Reserve Bank can quickly avail itself of its line(s) of credit to have other banks in the network support the dollar in the foreign exchange market. This would be for account of the Federal Reserve Bank of New York which, in this area, deals in both spot and future transactions. Detailed reports of Treasury and Federal Reserve foreign exchange operations appear in the *Monthly Review* of the Federal Reserve Bank of New York.

SPECIAL BONDS IN FOREIGN CURRENCIES

In 1961 another means used to protect the dollar against the threat of demands for convertibility into gold was the sale to foreign treasuries of U.S. interest-bearing, nonnegotiable securities redeemable in foreign currencies. In this way the rate of exchange is fixed—as far as the holder of the bonds is concerned—as the risk is assumed by the U.S. Treasury, which agrees to pay in foreign currency. These transactions enable the Treasury to increase temporarily its foreign exchange holdings and, in conjunction with Federal Reserve operations, to increase the resources available to the U.S. Government for large-scale intervention in the foreign exchange markets whenever necessary.

CONSULTATION AND COOPERATION AMONG CENTRAL BANKERS

Certain of the foregoing arrangements could not have been and would not be possible without close consultation and coordination among the central banks of the major countries. For example, the swap network could never have been arranged and could not function effectively and with appropriate mutual confidence unless there were continuous and close reviews to avoid conflicts of policy and operations. In these confrontations, some of which are bilateral and others of which take place through the Organization for Economic Cooperation and Development, officials of countries concerned must defend before their peers from other countries their Government's policies and attitudes, and especially its programs to remedy any undesirable developments. Such confrontations make for effective restraint on monetary and fiscal authorities. In a way it may be said that as an inducement to surplus countries not to cash in their chips for gold, the deficit countries must assure their peers that the discipline which would be imposed by such an action is recognized; and that appropriate corrective action is being undertaken which will at the same time maintain the corrective discipline under control and insure that the action taken will not be inordinately harmful to other countries.

Chapter XII

Commercial Banks and International Business

By far the more immediate and important banking services to international business in the short run are furnished by commercial banks, primarily those with established foreign departments. The number of U.S. banks that finance any sizable amount of international trade, with or without formal foreign (or international) departments, is not known, but 132 U.S. banks were members of the Bankers Association for Foreign Trade as of mid-1968. Membership in the association signifies an active interest and general participation in the financing of foreign trade.

Perhaps a more complete indication of the international activity of commercial banks is available from the monthly reports required by the Treasury Department in connection with U.S. banks' claims on and liabilities to foreigners.[1] This report must be submitted by all banks with liabilities to foreigners amounting to $500,000 or more, or with claims on foreigners amounting to $500,000 or more. The number of banks can vary, depending on the holdings,[2] but it is estimated that a little over 200 banks report to the Treasury each month under this requirement. Geographically, as of June 1967, these banks were located as shown in Exhibit 29.

Another statistical indication of the importance of this banking function is found in the summaries of these reports by bankers and banking institutions,

[1] Forms B1 and B2.

[2] The liabilities or claims must have averaged $500,000 over the preceding six months.

EXHIBIT 29

NUMBER OF BANKS IN THE UNITED STATES WHICH HAVE REPORTED SHORT-TERM CLAIMS ON FOREIGNERS ON TREASURY FOREIGN EXCHANGE FORM B-2, AS OF JUNE 30, 1967, BY STATE

State	Number	State	Number
Alabama	1	Minnesota	4
Arizona	2	Missouri	3
California	20	New Jersey	2
Connecticut	1	New York	79
District of Columbia	4	North Carolina	2
Florida	1	Ohio	8
Georgia	3	Oregon	3
Hawaii	2	Pennsylvania	9
Illinois	10	Rhode Island	2
Indiana	3	Tennessee	1
Kansas	2	Texas	14
Louisiana	3	Utah	1
Maryland	2	Virginia	1
Massachusetts	7	Washington	6
Michigan	6	Wisconsin	2
		All states and District of Columbia	204

Source: U.S. Treasury Department

which are published in the *Federal Reserve Bulletin.* As of February 1968, American banks reported $13,811 million in deposits due foreign banks and official institutions and $3,758 million in deposits due to all other foreigners. Short-term claims, on the other hand, totaled $8,534 million, the major elements of which were:[3]

Acceptances made for account of foreigners	$2,982 million
Loans to foreign banks and official institutions	$1,949 million
Loans to other foreigners	$1,215 million
Collections outstanding for own and customer accounts	$1,629 million

In the past few years there has also been a solid expansion of U.S. banking interests abroad in the form of branches, resident representatives, and direct affiliations. A recent survey showed that American banks have over 600 for-

[3] *Federal Reserve Bulletin,* Board of Governors, Federal Reserve System, Washington, D.C., May 1967, pp. 879, 883.

eign affiliates in 98 foreign countries and territories.[4] The functions performed for international business by commercial banks are several, and the remainder of this chapter will be devoted to a discussion of the more important ones.

Collection of drafts drawn by American exporters on foreign buyers or by foreign sellers on American buyers. This is one of the more important functions, since a very large part of foreign trade is financed by means of documentary drafts. The shipper retains effective control over the merchandise through the normal practice of instructing his bank—which, in turn, instructs its branch or correspondent—not to release the bill of lading (or perhaps other documents as well) until the draft has been honored by payment or acceptance. Use of such drafts also benefits the buyer of the goods. First of all, he does not have to advance funds with his order or pay the cost of a letter of credit. Then, by being able to examine the documents attached to the draft, he has practical evidence prior to payment or acceptance that the seller has provided him with a bill of lading and other documents called for in the contract.

Drafts on foreigners in process of collection represent obligations arising from a variety of transactions, but the larger part represents exports of merchandise. Because drafts in process of collection represent a normal "float" of drafts not yet due as well as those due on presentation, plus overdue items, it is not possible to relate accurately the outstanding draft volume with the volume of commercial exports.

Discounting or purchasing of drafts drawn by American exporters on foreign debtors. In normal practice, drafts are discounted with recourse to the exporter or drawer of the draft who endorses it. When purchased outright, which occurs far less frequently, there is no recourse to the exporter or drawer. Commercial banks may be said to be encouraged in the discounting and purchasing of drafts arising from American exports through special facilities of the Export-Import Bank. This bank issues guarantees to commercial banks against foreign commercial and political risks related to *medium-term* export transactions being financed by banks on a nonrecourse basis. And, beginning in 1966, the Export-Import Bank arranged for direct advances to commercial banks to encourage them to finance U.S. exports by relating such advances to the bank's holding of customer paper arising from exports and having a maturity of more than 180 days. Loans were originally made by the Export-Import Bank against those holdings arising from exports made on or after March 1, 1966. Subsequently, it was arranged that additional advances would be available on the basis of the increase in the commercial bank's export paper portfolio over what it was on the preceding September 1.

[4] *International Commerce Magazine,* U.S. Department of Commerce, Washington, D.C., September 11, 1967, p. 11.

Purchase and sale of foreign exchange. This includes not only the purchase of drafts or cheques[5] issued by foreign banks or of cheques drawn on them or of drafts drawn on foreign firms (bills of exchange), but also the purchase and sale of foreign currencies, which are of some importance to travelers leaving or entering this country. A very important aspect of this function consists of the sale of drafts or cable transfers drawn against the American bank's accounts abroad. For example, if one needs a draft or cable transfer payable in pounds, or yen, or francs, the place to obtain it is a commercial bank which carries accounts in those currencies or which has correspondents through which such foreign exchange transactions can be arranged. The bank's deposits in foreign currencies thus constitute a pool out of which international trade is actually financed. It is constantly being replenished by the purchase of immediate and forward instruments denominated in foreign currency and arising from exports of goods or services, from investment income, or from other claims that accrue to mainly private U.S. interests. These interests, of course, want dollars in exchange for what they have acquired abroad. And the pool is constantly being drawn on by the demands of numerous private businesses or individuals who must pay for imports of goods and services, or pay in currencies other than the dollar in settlement of the many other transactions that represent international commerce.

Actually, each bank active in the field maintains a predetermined inventory position in several foreign currencies (naturally subject to constant change with changing conditions), which consists of funds immediately available or coming due at a future date. Against this, the bank meets the requirements of its customers for spot and forward purchases; and it stands ready to give dollars to its customers for their spot and forward claims on foreigners acquired through various business transactions. And if the bank does not have available the foreign exchange its customers require, it will buy the exchange from the market to satisfy the customer's needs. On the other hand, if the bank acquires from its customers more foreign exchange of any type than it anticipates needing, it will reduce its inventory of such exchange on that date by selling it on the market. The term "foreign exchange market" is used liberally, as there is no one, central, formally organized marketplace. Instead, the market consists primarily of a few brokers and dealers in New York and the foreign departments of commercial banks as well as the Federal Reserve Bank of New York. Similar "markets" exist in other money centers, such as London, Zurich, and Beirut.

Commercial banks in the United States are thus the place where practically all of the foreign exchange earnings of American business are converted into dollars, and banks abroad are the place where dollars earned by

[5] "Cheques" is the spelling used in most countries, while in the United States it is "checks."

foreigners are converted into foreign currencies. These exchanges are effected through the deposit accounts maintained internationally—quite commonly between pairs of correspondent banks. Transactions are in spot (immediate transfer by cable or mail) and in future contracts, and there is no possibility of exhausting the supply of foreign exchange unless there is government restriction which amounts to inconvertibility. The price of the exchange will be affected by the relative scarcity or abundance of each and will be influenced, if not controlled within permissible limits, by government intervention.

Issuance of letters of credit. The function of collecting drafts does not in itself provide bank financing; here the credit is extended to the buyer by the seller. But, as often happens, either the buyer's individual credit standing (including conditions in his country) or customs of the trade suggest the use of a commercial letter of credit issued by a bank experienced and active in foreign trade financing. Commercial letters of credit have the attribute of substituting a bank's credit standing for that of the buyer. Hence the buyer, by making this arrangement which practically eliminates the commercial credit risk, is in a position to obtain the most favorable price for the goods he is buying. And the seller, by being able to offer an asset of high credibility, is able to obtain financing at the most advantageous rate for private credit; and this perhaps in a money market different from his own.

In addition to having his risk practically eliminated, the seller, by retaining effective control of the documents until the draft is honored,[6] also has the assurance that documents accompanying the draft will be carefully checked to guard against error. The buyer, in addition to being in the best position for price advantage, has the assurance of careful checking of documents on which he relies as evidence that what is called for in his purchase contract has, in fact, been done. But, as stated earlier, documents do not *guarantee* that all this has been done. What the documents say, fundamentally, is that goods called for in the letter of credit are purported to have been shipped properly.

In addition to commercial letters of credit, banks also issue travelers' letters of credit. These are generally for sizable amounts, and they are associated with books of indication which specify the correspondent banks abroad that will honor drafts drawn against the letter as needed. They have some advantage over the usual travelers' checks in that they are not as bulky for the same amount of funds. The traveler's letter of credit is especially useful for a person on a long buying trip who will be making relatively few but large-volume purchases.

The cost of a commercial letter of credit to the requester is usually one-eighth of 1 percent per month (1.5 percent per year). For this, the buyer in

[6] This is done by the use of documents attached to the draft.

the United States is able to offer an exporter abroad the right to draw a sight draft, payable by a bank at once, or a time draft which, upon acceptance by the contracting bank, becomes a banker's acceptance.

Typically, a bank is requested to open a letter of credit by the importer (or the importer's bank), although the demand for letter-of-credit financing of goods in storage in the United States or abroad, or goods moving between foreign countries, will originate from other functional interests in international trade. In any case, letters of credit are *one* means of commercial bank financing to which international business has access. In all cases, regardless of the method of financing used, the customer must satisfy the bank as to his credit-worthiness. A letter of credit is a contingent rather than an actual liability of a bank.[7] It does not become *actual* until its conditions have been met, at which time the draft is either paid or accepted. Statistics are not maintained on the volume of letters of credit issued; they relate only to acceptances outstanding.

Acceptance of drafts drawn under letter of credit. The creation of acceptances by banks constitutes a valuable financing aid to foreign trade. It substitutes the bank's reputation for that of a business firm, and since relatively few, but experienced, banks are truly active in this field, the quality of acceptances is such that their owners can convert them into cash at a most favorable discount rate. The ability of national banks to accept such drafts (thereby creating liabilities for themselves) derives from the Federal Reserve Act of 1913 (Section 13). The volume of such acceptances varies with the volume of international trade, which constitutes its major basis, as well as with the demand for acceptances to create dollar exchange and to finance goods in storage. Acceptances valued at $1,730 million were reported in 1929, of which 80 percent was based on international trade and 20 percent was of domestic origin. The total fell to $233 million in 1939 and did not show any significant growth again until the late 1950's. By 1960 the total amount reported was over $2 billion, and this figure continued to expand to over $4 billion in mid-1968.[8]

The Federal Reserve Bank of New York publishes a *Monthly Acceptance Survey* indicating the volume of acceptances outstanding and the basis

[7] For details as to rights and liabilities under letters of credit, see *Uniform Customs and Practices for Commercial Documentary Credits,* International Chamber of Commerce, Paris, 1962; Ernest Shaw, *Practical Aspects of Commercial Letters of Credit,* Irving Trust Company, New York, 1967; and William Ward and Henry Harfield, *Bank Credits and Acceptances,* The Ronald Press Company, New York, 1948.

[8] See Robert L. Cooper, "Bankers' Acceptances," *Monthly Review,* the Federal Reserve Bank of New York, June 1966, and later monthly acceptance surveys reported by the Federal Reserve Bank of New York.

on which they were created. As of the end of February 1968, the total amount reported was $4,266 million, based as follows:[9]

On imports	$1,091 million
On exports	$1,029 million
On goods stored in or shipped between foreign countries	$1,979 million
To create dollar exchange	$ 33 million
On domestic shipments and storage	$ 134 million

The foregoing tabulation shows that almost all of the acceptances were created in response to demands having an international base. However, it is not known, nor can it be reliably estimated, what proportion of American export and import trade is financed by this mechanism.

Once an acceptance is created, it becomes a definite liability of a bank and a definite asset of the payee or of the person to whom it is endorsed. The owner can then discount the acceptance at a very favorable rate—as of mid-1968, the going rate was from 5.87 to 6 percent on acceptances with a maturity of 31 to 90 days. This compared favorably with and, in fact, was noticeably lower than bank rates on short-term business loans as reported by banks at the same time, when the prime rate was 6.5 percent. The important point here, as suggested earlier, is that many of the companies that can qualify for letter-of-credit/acceptance financing are not able to qualify for the prime rate on direct loans, which is given only to the stronger borrowers in the United States and normally on larger loans. Acceptances are commonly for relatively small, uneven amounts.

The existence of acceptance markets in London and New York, where rates are relatively at their lowest, and the eligibility of American bankers' acceptances for purchase or discount by the Federal Reserve have a lot to do with the financing of third-country world trade in sterling and dollars. Another reason for the dominance of these currencies in financing trade is the existence of a large number of foreign branches and affiliates of European and American banks in other countries. These provide a body of experience specialized in international trade financing that cannot be matched by primarily domestically oriented institutions.

Purchase and sale of acceptances. Letters of credit provide no actual funds for financing, nor do acceptances. But acceptances, which are a bank obligation, are an instrument that can be converted into cash at a very favor-

[9] *Monthly Acceptance Survey,* Federal Reserve Bank of New York, March 19, 1968.

able rate of discount and on short notice. It is by disposing of the acceptances that funds come into the hands of the exporter or of the payee of the draft on which the acceptance rests.

In New York acceptances are bought and sold primarily by five or six dealers who make a market for them. In recent years some of the larger stock exchange firms have entered the market as middlemen.[10] Commercial banks are also among the active buyers and sellers of acceptances, including their own. In the latter case the purchase (or discount) is direct, and a dealer is not involved. And, of course, a bank will discount directly for its own customers the acceptances of other recognized banks held by the customer.

When a bank creates an acceptance, the acceptance belongs not to the bank but to the payee or person to whom it has been endorsed. But this person probably wants money—not a bank promise to pay out money in the future. So it is standard practice for the bank to discount its own acceptance (which is its liability) for its customer. At that time, the nature of the bank's asset and liability changes; it now owes money, payable in the future, to itself. It has, in fact, advanced its own funds to the owner of the acceptance. Accordingly, regulations for reporting the bank's condition require that customers' liabilities on acceptances outstanding not include acceptances held by the creating bank itself; such transactions are now to be reported as loans and discounts because they are a direct advance of funds.

The extent to which banks buy their own acceptances is influenced by money-market conditions. As of a fairly recent date, December 31, 1966, acceptances outstanding were reported by the Federal Reserve Bank of New York in its *Monthly Acceptance Survey* as amounting to $3,603 million. But at the same date, acceptances outstanding—that is, not held by the creating bank—as reported by the Federal Deposit Insurance Corporation were $2,314 million.[11] Thus it appears that as of that time a substantial portion of the acceptances created were bought by the creating banks themselves. Commercial banks are thus a vital part of the market for acceptances after they have been created.

Direct loans to companies engaged in foreign trade, without use of specialized international financing instruments. As mentioned earlier, letters of credit are only *one* method of financing foreign trade, but a highly specialized one. Many companies find it advantageous or even necessary to sell abroad on open account, carrying the receivables themselves. In this case it may, and probably will, be necessary for them to obtain short-term financing for the purpose, just as they must for carrying domestic receivables. Com-

[10] For example, Merrill Lynch, Pierce, Fenner and Smith, and other firms.

[11] Report of Call No. 78, Federal Deposit Insurance Corporation, Washington, D.C., December 31, 1966.

mercial banks thus extend lines of credit to domestic producers and exporters, which in turn can then extend credit abroad on their own account.

Factoring. A postwar phenomenon in the financing of foreign trade by commercial banks is the appearance of a factoring mechanism. This is a facility that seems to have been first emphasized by the First National Bank of Boston but which is now available through a few more banks. Factoring particularly helps credit checking and collection abroad by establishment of a network of banks joined for that purpose, and it is claimed that the arrangement permits more liberal credit terms and faster decisions on orders than would otherwise be possible. Furthermore, the competitive drive for exports has led buyers to demand trade credit on open terms. Approval of the credit by a factor (or his representative) in a foreign country facilitates acceptance of the order and establishment of the receivable. But, again, this does not in itself actually provide funds. If advances against the accounts receivable are desired by the exporter, he pays interest for the advance over and above the modest service fee he pays for the factoring. Collection of the receivables is undertaken by the factor in the buyer's own country, and the buyer is normally instructed by invoice to pay the factor.

Provision of economic and credit intelligence. Banks active in international business, through their constant contact with certain foreign markets and through branches or correspondent networks, are in a unique position to provide their customers with up-to-date intelligence on economic conditions in the countries in which they are active. They are also in a position to advise on the credit standing and reputation of individual firms in these countries. Similarly, intelligence is needed on commodities or other products. Some banks are in an excellent position to provide or assist with such intelligence because of immediate experience or regular contact with branches and correspondents.

A constant requirement of sellers, either on new or on repeat orders, is credit checking of the buyers. This is so because credit conditions constantly change. Banks are traditionally used as credit references, and they will exchange credit information with each other internationally that might not be forthcoming if the inquirer were a business firm. Banks can contact the foreign firm's bank, directly or secondarily, and obtain the information needed for their American customers. Credit checking is one of the more fundamental yet sometimes insufficiently recognized functions performed for international business by commercial banks.

Assistance to exporters and importers in finding suitable business counterparts abroad. Closely related to the exchange of credit information concerning customers is the knowledge that banks have, or can quickly obtain, about companies in their areas of operation that might be looking for or would consider opportunities to do new business. A firm considering entry into a new territory would be well advised to see its bank for help in locating a desirable counterpart in the particular foreign country. Provision of such names cannot, of course, burden the bank with liability; but one can feel assured that suggestion of a name or names implies that the available information is favorable.

Processing of government letters of commitment. The procedure by which American exporters obtain funds to cover exports to foreign recipients of the Agency for International Development is through having letters of credit issued in their favor by American banks that have been designated as recipients of AID letters of commitment. Exporters can then draw drafts against the bank as authorized by its letter of credit. A somewhat comparable procedure has been established for exports under the Agricultural Trade Development and Assistance Act of 1954 (Public Law 480). The Commodity Credit Corporation issues letters of commitment to the U.S. bank or banks selected by the foreign importing country or private trade entity.

Banks in other countries perform substantially the same or reciprocal functions for their customers, plus others, such as equity participation, in which American banks may not legally engage. However, some American banks, through the medium of Edge Act corporations, have been able to offer a wider range of services to international business than may be offered under the usual charters.

It should be obvious from the foregoing discussion that commercial banks have a most important function to perform in the financing of international business. One would be hard put to conclude that there can be for any appreciable time any shortage of financing capacity from a commercial point of view, unless such transactions are impeded by government policy.

Appendix A

Statistical Systems and Publications

The classification systems employed in international trade are complex because there are literally thousands of products that enter world trade. Many of these products' categories must be subdivided to be of use to business and, at the same time, must lend themselves to being grouped and aggregated, according to the desired characteristic, to facilitate broader economic analysis and comparisons to satisfy the differing requirements of users of the statistics.

STATISTICAL SYSTEMS

Statistical subdivisions and aggregates are only the beginning; they serve to *identify* a particular product or to establish a particular group or category of products. What the businessman and market analyst need to know about international activity in the product depends on the nature of their business or interest. It may have to do with production, with consumption, with international trade, or possibly with each of these. In the matter of international trade, which is the primary interest here, it is necessary, in order to satisfy the varied demands, to provide a statistical system that will yield for each identified product, and also for aggregates, information about exports or imports along the following lines:

- By country of destination or origin.
- By method of transport, whether by air or by ocean—that is, by liner or tramp tanker, United States or foreign.

- By trade route.
- By coastal district.
- By port of entry or exit.

Information is given for any or all of these subjects by value and volume within individual and cumulative time periods. The origin and design of statistical systems thus constitute a major task for govenments, for trade associations, or for businesses. It is common to have these units working cooperatively to develop and improve a system that will ease the burden and will serve the needs of all affected interests—that is, the suppliers of primary data and the users of aggregates from whatever view their compilation seeks to satisfy.

Origin and systematization of statistics in foreign trade. In international trade all of the accumulated commercial statistics must be developed from basic documents executed by those charged with responsibility for reporting the primary data. Basic documents in the United States are the Shipper's Export Declaration (of which there are about 800,000 per month) and the Import Entry (of which there are about 250,000 per month). These documents are filed with the U.S. Bureau of Customs as a requirement for each export or import transaction. They are in turn submitted to the Bureau of the Census, where they are coded and entered on punched cards or magnetic tapes for electronic data processing.

Tariff Schedules of the United States (TSUS). The classification systems employed by the collecting and reporting agency of the government must, as suggested earlier, be designed to satisfy the needs of several end-uses. For example, in the case of imports, one of the first is revenue purposes, and for this purpose the United States employs a classification system known as Tariff Schedules of the United States (TSUS). It is, in fact, the official schedule according to which duties are levied, and, since it is the basis for revenue, it has been approved by the Congress to give it legal stature. The TSUS contains a little over 6,300 different product identifications, and its purpose is to facilitate the determination of duty status and the collection of such duty, if any.

Finer detail needed for market research purposes. The TSUS, while serving its basic purpose without difficulty, does not provide adequate detail for commercial intelligence nor for rearrangement into the several aggregates needed for broader economic analysis and comparisons. Therefore, in order to obtain the wealth of data needed for commercial purposes, and to permit better comparability with other systems, the TSUS has been further subdivided into some 10,000 items (of which some 1,200 are textile product classifications), each identifiable by an assigned statistical number. This constitutes the Tariff Schedules of the United States, Annotated (TSUSA). These items are sometimes referred to by Census Bureau experts as "building blocks" in international trade statistics; they can be rearranged or shuffled to yield detail or aggregates according to the characteristic it is desired to emphasize. This detail and flexibility are what make it possible to better analyze trade with foreign markets of precise interest to the businessman and to better study competition abroad. TSUSA is the most detailed breakdown for imports available to U.S. foreign traders.

Export classification system (Schedule B). The same detailed classification schedule and breakdown are not used by the United States for both imports and exports, primarily because of the different composition of the trade and the fact that the import schedule had to be fitted to the legal requirements of the Tariff Act. Yet reasonable concordance between import and export statistics is required because of the need to compare both imports and exports with production, the statistics of which are under a still different classification system. For exports, the U.S. classification system is known as Schedule B, Revised, and it contains some 3,600 seven-digit codes. These codes, too, can be rearranged and grouped into aggregates so that one can compare both exports and imports in terms of categories, if not in detail. The Schedule B classification is the finest detail in which U.S. exports are reported statistically.

The Brussels Tariff Nomenclature (BTN). The TSUS was designed by the United States solely to satisfy its own needs. Other countries have similarly developed national schedules for tariffs, and there has been some move toward international uniformity in tariff schedules. The greatest accomplishment in this respect is the Brussels Tariff Nomenclature (BTN), which was adopted in 1955. As of April 1967, it was employed as the basis for classifying products for imposition of duties by over 110 countries and customs territories.

The BTN consists of about 1,100 four-digit headings arranged in 99 chapters, which are themselves grouped into 21 sections. In general, goods are grouped according to the material out of which they are made, and most chapters are developed "progressively," that is, starting from raw materials and progressing to finished articles.[1] It is specifically designed for customs tariff purposes, and each country using the agreed classification is free to employ subheadings under the agreed headings to accommodate national needs. For example, the Benelux countries employ about 2,800 total positions; Italy uses about 7,600; and the common external tariff of the EEC

[1] *The Customs Cooperation Council,* The Customs Cooperation Council, Brussels, 1964, p. 15.

uses about 2,800. The classification itself does not establish or indicate rates of duty since each country is able to set its own duty on each position. But the existence of such a system means that an exporter can, once a product is identified and its classification has been established, more readily determine the applicable duty rate for a given country and the comparable duty rates as between different countries. The BTN is the customs classification system used for tariff purposes in the European Economic Community (EEC), the European Free Trade Association (EFTA), and the Latin American Free Trade Association (LAFTA). Not only does international uniformity of tariff classification thus facilitate world trade, it also provides a common customs language, which facilitates tariff negotiations.

International comparability needed for analysis. In the BTN, as mentioned previously, articles are grouped primarily according to the nature of the material out of which they are made. But commercial intelligence and other economic and statistical analyses require groupings of articles on the basis of classes of goods, such as food, raw materials, chemicals, machinery, and transport equipment, and also by the state of fabrication and industrial origin. In other words, comparability is needed according to the stage or grouping in which the product is traded internationally. Therefore, a different, or companion, system to the BTN had to be devised.

Standard International Trade Classification (SITC), Revised. The search for greater comparability of foreign trade statistics has been a long one. The problem drew the attention of the League of Nations, which formed a committee known as the Committee of Statistical Experts, and later of the United Nations, whose Statistical Commission drew up the United Nations Standard International Trade Classification in 1950. Governments were encouraged by the Economic and Social Council of the United Nations to adopt the standard system of classification, with such modifications as may have been necessary to meet national requirements and to rearrange their statistical data in accordance with this system for purposes of international comparison.

Since many European countries were employing the BTN of the Customs Cooperation Council for tariff purposes, it became necessary to regroup its subheadings or the other national details in some way if market and economic analyses were to be facilitated. Consequently, a group of experts interested in the problem drew up a proposal to match the original SITC and the BTN; the result is now known as the SITC, Revised. Under this classification, by the use of five-digit headings, a reciprocal one-to-one correspondence was achieved between the SITC, Revised and the BTN. Consequently, widespread adoption of the SITC, Revised as the basis for reporting statistics on international trade to the international organizations, the

United Nations in particular, as well as its obvious advantages for market research and economic analyses, led to the United States' decision to publish its own foreign statistics under three-digit SITC group headings in 1963 and then subsequently in terms of the revised Schedules A and B, both of which are structured according to the SITC.[2]

Internationally, then, foreign trade statistics are collected and presented according to one major, widely used classification—the Standard International Trade Classification, Revised—and according to the several individual national systems. The important development is that the intelligence on a comparable basis is now available, and, for the first time, there is a widely agreed international classification for international trade, which makes possible market studies that were only a dream as recently as the early 1960's.

Accessibility of statistics. Publication of statistical data is expensive, and much of the information desired is highly specialized and compartmentalized, such as commodity trade with one country or trade in one commodity but with several countries, and this is commonly arranged according to method of transportation, customs district, and so forth. Moreover, if the public had to wait for all this data to be published, the intelligence conveyed might often be stale by weeks or months. Hence the publications program is limited, but availability of the statistics must not be delayed. Accordingly, detailed, machine-run tabulations containing the basic import and export data, prepared but not published, are immediately available for reference by selected Department of Commerce offices; and copies of these runs, in whole or in part, are available to subscribers on a timely basis. Other reference tabulations are similarly available shortly thereafter.

There are two main suppliers of statistics on international trade: first, the United States Department of Commerce (Bureau of Census) for statistics pertaining to foreign trade of the United States; and second, the United Nations for statistics pertaining to the foreign trade of any or all countries reporting to it. The United Nations publishes data in detail only as fine as five-digit SITC, Revised, but most foreign countries collect it in finer detail and sometimes publish these details. As of 1966, almost 70 countries were reporting their commodity-by-country trade data to the United Nations Statistical Office in five-digit SITC, Revised, detail (they either report on this basis or on another which can be converted); and for about 30 others the data are available in four-digit or three-digit detail. Some

[2] See, for reference, *Foreign Trade Report FT 135* and *Foreign Trade Report FT 410,* the reports in which United States trade statistics are published. See, also, for example, code 725.01 (domestic electrical refrigerators) which appears in the SITC and is also used in Schedule A and Schedule B.

countries report export trade only, and others import trade only; and some report exports and imports in different detail. But not all countries report their statistics on the same urgent time schedule. Some reports become available three or four months after the fact; others not before six to nine months.

PUBLICATIONS

Statistical publications pertaining to foreign trade are voluminous, whether issued by the United States, by foreign governments, or by international bodies. A text of this type is no place to attempt to list them; moreover, the supply or variety changes frequently. Yet it will be relevant to identify some of the more basic ones.

U.S. statistical publications. The two most basic publications of U.S. foreign trade statistics, with commodity by country of origin or destination detail, are: (1) *Foreign Trade Report FT 135*—imports, commodity by country of origin; and (2) *Foreign Trade Report FT 410*—exports, commodity by country of destination. Both of these appear monthly and contain both monthly and cumulative year-to-date data. They are available at any field office of the U.S. Department of Commerce.

Time series of a more general nature are published in brochure form, monthly, under the title *United States Foreign Trade* (for the year or years concerned). This is one of the Department of Commerce publications appearing in a series called *Overseas Business Reports.* These time series show total exports and imports, foreign trade in selected major commodities, and exports and imports by country but not cross-related as to commodities. Time series of various specifications are also available in the annual *Statistical Abstract of the United States.*

International statistical publications. There are numerous international publications, monthly, quarterly, and annual, which pertain to foreign trade of the world. These are issued by such organizations as the United Nations, the International Monetary Fund, the International Bank for Reconstruction and Development, the Food and Agriculture Organization, the Organization for Economic Cooperation and Development, the European Economic Community, the European Free Trade Association, and so forth. The following selected examples are among the more useful publications:

1. *Direction of Trade* (joint UN, IMF, IBRD). Monthly and cumulative for year, showing trade by country in U.S. currency. Arrangement is export total by destination and import total by

origin; no commodity detail; about 120 reporting countries, plus selected groupings.

2. *Commodity Trade Statistics* (UN). Published throughout the year by country as quarterly data for that country become available. Shows for reporting country imports by country of origin and exports by country of destination, where volume was $100,000 or more; in SITC one-digit to selected five-digit commodity detail; about 50 reporting countries.
3. *Yearbook of International Trade Statistics* (UN). Annual, showing data for about four years on value and weight. Shows trade by principal country of origin or destination, but not subdivided by commodity; and shows exports and imports by commodity, but not subdivided by country.
4. *World Trade Annual* (prepared by UN; published by Walker and Company, New York). First published in 1964, covering 1963 data for 22 countries. The 1966 edition covered 24 countries. Covers commodity trade in five-digit SITC detail between a reporting country and its trading partners if its value was $50,000 or more. Data for those countries not reporting are reflected in the statistics of those that do report. Only data between nonreporting countries are not represented.
5. *Statistical Bulletins,* especially Series C, "Trade by Commodities," quarterly, (OECD). Shows quantity and value (value in U.S. currency); data for each OECD country give tabulations for about 575 four-digit SITC subgroups, showing country of destination or origin. Details are given for every country of destination, if the amount going to any single one exceeds either $50,000 or 10 percent of the reporting country's exports of that product; and on imports, for every country of origin, if the amount coming from any source exceeds either $25,000 or 10 percent of the reporting country's total imports of that product.
6. *EEC Foreign Trade Analytical Tables.* Annual, for each EEC country and EEC total. Gives full breakdown, by areas and countries of origin or destination, for all five-digit SITC items when the trade with any country of destination or origin amounts to $10,000 or more for that item. Values are in U.S. currency.

Many other publications are issued for special purposes, usually with more restricted commodity or area coverage or concentrating on some particular aspect of the commerce, such as method of transporation.

Appendix B

International Business Intelligence Sources

Regardless of the size of a company and its degree of commitment, the officer or officers in charge must have background information on international business as a broad subject as well as be informed about the narrower market (product or geographic) in which the company operates. The actual interest in and need for this type of intelligence are borne out by wide attendance and participation each year in several world trade conferences and by business support and participation in seminars and briefing sessions on the subject sponsored by the American Management Association.

To be useful, this intelligence must be kept up to date, which may be accomplished by reading or scanning everything that comes across the desk (a nearly impossible task) or by selective reading and timely use of adequate and appropriate reference sources. The material suggested here is partly what may be called standard references, such as annual editions, and partly current literature, ranging from monthly to daily publications and, in some cases, only occasional publications. The references and services listed below might profitably be looked into to ascertain whether their coverage and approach are what is desired. Some of the references are quite expensive, while the cost of others is very moderate or free.

GENERAL BACKGROUND

A good, working reference shelf should include some of the following:

- *Business Abroad* (Dun & Bradstreet Publications).

- *Business International* (Business International).
- *The Columbia Journal of World Business* (distributed by Pergamon Press).
- *Custom House Guide* (Budd Publications).
- *Exporters' Encyclopedia* (Dun & Bradstreet Publications).
- *Foreign Trade Service* (Chase Manhattan Bank).
- *International Commerce Magazine* (U.S. Department of Commerce).
- *International Management* (McGraw-Hill Book Company).
- *International Trade Forum* (GATT).
- *International Trade Information* (Bank of America).
- *The Journal of Commerce.*
- *Minerals Yearbook, Volume IV* (U.S. Department of Interior).
- *Monthly Bulletin of Agricultural Economics and Statistics* (FAO).
- *OECD Observer* (OECD).
- *Penetrating the International Market* (American Management Association).
- *Profit Potential in the Developing Countries* (American Management Association).
- *Purchasing in Worldwide Operations* (American Management Association).
- *The Wall Street Journal.*
- *World Business* (Chase Manhattan Bank).
- *Worldwide P&I Planning* (Intercontinental Publications).

BACKGROUND ON OPERATIONS

On the problems of price quotations, in order to clarify the responsibility of the seller and the buyer, one might refer to:

- *Incoterms* (International Chamber of Commerce).
- *Revised American Foreign Trade Definitions* (National Foreign Trade Council; Chamber of Commerce of the United States; American Importers Association).

On the special role of documents and financing procedures:

- *Banker's Guide to Financing Exports* (American Bankers Association).

- *Export and Import Procedures* (Morgan Guaranty Trust Company).
- *Financing International Operations* (American Management Association).
- *Uniform Customs and Practices for Documentary Credits* (International Chamber of Commerce).

On credit insurance availability and procedures:

- *Guide to Credit Insurance* (Foreign Credit Insurance Association).

On special services and functions:

- *Foreign Commerce Handbook* (Chamber of Commerce of the United States).
- *Introduction to Doing Export-Import Business* (Chamber of Commerce of the United States).

BACKGROUND DATA AND CURRENT INDICATORS (FOCUSED ON COUNTRY)

- *Board of Trade Journal* (United Kingdom Board of Trade).
- *Clipper Cargo Horizons* (Pan American World Airways).
- *First Person Overseas Reports* (First National Bank of Boston).
- *Foreign Information Service* (First National City Bank).
- Foreign Markets Reports Service (U.S. Department of Commerce).
- *Foreign Trade Service* (Chase Manhattan Bank).
- *International Commerce Magazine* (U.S. Department of Commerce).
- *International Financial Statistics* (IMF and IBRD).
- *International Trade Information* (Bank of America).
- *International Notes* (Chemical Bank New York Trust Company).
- *Market Air Newsletter* (Trans World Airlines).
- *Overseas Business Reports* (U.S. Department of Commerce).
- *Overseas Survey* (Barclays Bank, D.C.O.).
- *World Business* (Chase Manhattan Bank).

TYPICAL PUBLICATIONS WITH NATIONAL OR REGIONAL ORIENTATION

- *African News Digest* (Farrell Lines).
- *Belgian Trade Review* (Belgian Chamber of Commerce in the United States).
- *Commerce in France* (American Chamber of Commerce in France).
- *Doing Business in and with Australia* (American Management Association).
- *Doing Business in Mexico* (American Management Association).
- *The European Common Market* (American Management Association).
- *Far Eastern Economist.*
- *Foreign Trade* (Canadian Department of Trade and Commerce).
- *German-American Trade News* (German-American Chambers of Commerce in New York and Chicago).
- *Pacific Commerce.*

Also: For tariff guides, customs journals on individual foreign countries may be purchased from Federal Clearinghouse for Scientific and Technical Information, Springfield, Virginia 22151.

FOCUS ON FOREIGN MARKETS FOR PRODUCTS AND ON COMPANIES ABROAD

- *Dun & Bradstreet Reference Book* and *Dun & Bradstreet Register* (reference data on individual firms abroad—Dun & Bradstreet Publications).
- Foreign Market Reports Service (U.S. Department of Commerce).
- *International Commerce Magazine* (U.S. Department of Commerce).
- *The International Market Guide* (Dun & Bradstreet Publications).
- *International Reports* (International Reports).
- Local bank.
- Local chamber of commerce or trade association.
- Others in the business.

- *Overseas Business Reports* (U.S. Department of Commerce).
- *Trade Lists* (U.S. Department of Commerce).
- World Trade Directory Reports (U.S. Department of Commerce).

BACKGROUND DATA ESPECIALLY APPLICABLE TO THE UNITED STATES

Every American company is immediately affected by American policies, as reflected in laws and regulations, and by conditions in the domestic economy. Literature pertaining to these matters is so extensive and transitory as to preclude anything but a highly selective listing of reference suggestions, which is as follows:

- *Survey of Current Business* (U.S. Department of Commerce). A weekly publication which includes the official quarterly reports on the balance of payments and the annual survey of investments abroad, as well as special occasional articles pertaining to the overall international business of the United States.
- *International Commerce Magazine* (U.S. Department of Commerce). A weekly magazine based primarily on reports received from the Foreign Service posts and from Department of Commerce offices abroad, such as trade centers. The magazine contains references to such categories of intelligence as U.S. Government actions, foreign government actions affecting trade or business opportunities, investment opportunities, world trade opportunities, and miscellaneous articles of a broad, usually geographic nature.
- *Department of State Bulletin* (U.S. Department of State). A monthly publication incorporating official reports or notices on U.S. Government participation in international conferences, many of which pertain to trade policy or to commodity arrangements or to international organizations the activity of which affects international business opportunities.
- *Foreign Agriculture* (Department of Agriculture). A magazine dealing mainly with international trade in primary agricultural commodities.
- *Tariff Schedules of the United States, Annotated* (TSUSA). Specifies the tariff rates and other import regulations pertaining to each individual product entering into American import trade.

- *Comprehensive Export Schedule* and supplementary *Current Export Bulletin* (U.S. Department of Commerce). Describes the control system pertaining to exports from the United States, including the designation of products requiring licenses and the destinations to which exports must be licensed.

Index